Categories

122 Thematic Vocabulary Lessons

By Barbara Gregorich

J. Weston Walch, Publisher
Portland, Maine

Users' Guide
to
Walch Reproducible Books

As part of our general effort to provide educational materials which are as practical and economical as possible, we have designated this publication a "reproducible book." The designation means that purchase of the book includes purchase of the right to limited reproduction of all pages on which this symbol appears:

Here is the basic Walch policy: We grant to individual purchasers of this book the right to make sufficient copies of reproducible pages for use by all students of a single teacher. This permission is limited to a single teacher, and does not apply to entire schools or school systems, so institutions purchasing the book should pass the permission on to a single teacher. Copying of the book or its parts for resale is prohibited.

Any questions regarding this policy or requests to purchase further reproduction rights should be addressed to:

Permissions Editor
J. Weston Walch, Publisher
P.O. Box 658
Portland, ME 04104-0658

—J. Weston Walch, Publisher

2 3 4 5 6 7 8 9 10

ISBN 0-8251-2415-8

Printed in the United States of America

Contents

Teacher's Guide

Reproducible Student Masters

Section Six — *Clothing*

Section Seven — *Transportation*

Section Eight — *Machines and Tools*

To the Teacher

Categories helps students in three different ways: (1) it helps increase the number of vocabulary words they know the meaning of; (2) it helps them learn the extent of information available in a dictionary; (3) it helps expand their general knowledge about broad categories of subject matter.

Sections. *Categories* is divided into eleven sections that cover a broad range of categories: (1) The Universe and the Earth; (2) Plants; (3) Animals; (4) The Human Body; (5) Houses and Other Shelters; (6) Clothing; (7) Transportation; (8) Machines and Tools; (9) Sports and Recreation; (10) Information and Entertainment; (11) Social Institutions.

Activity Pages. These eleven categories contain a total of 122 activity pages. The activity pages have been designed to include a wide variety of activities: word wheels, fill-in-the-blank, multiple choice, phonic spellings, find the hidden words, replace the words in a story, matching, true-false, rhyming words, making compound words, unscrambling words, classifying terms, and others. The activity pages may be done in class or assigned as homework. Each activity page also includes an extra activity that you may either assign as homework or as a project to be completed by groups during class.

All activity pages are self-contained. It is not necessary to use them in the order they are given, nor is it necessary to go through the sections in the order they are given.

Difficulty Level. Each of the eleven sections contains activity pages that vary in difficulty. At the top right-hand side of each page is a code that rates the difficulty level. ✎ stands for easy; ✎✎ stands for medium difficulty; ✎✎✎ stands for challenging. You may use the activity pages in the order they are numbered—in that case, your students will receive worksheets of varying difficulty as they go through the book. Or you may wish to sort the activity pages within each section in an order of increasing difficulty. Or you may wish to use worksheets of only one difficulty level. It is up to you to decide what will work best for your students.

On the next page is a chart listing the worksheets in degrees of difficulty, from Easy to Medium to Challenging.

SECTION	EASY	MEDIUM	DIFFICULT
One	6, 7, 10	1, 2, 4, 5, 9	3, 8
Two	17, 18, 22	13, 15, 21	11, 12, 14, 16, 19, 20
Three	25, 30, 32, 34, 36	23, 27, 29, 35	24, 26, 28, 31, 33, 37
Four	38, 41, 42	39, 40, 45	43, 44, 46, 47
Five	48, 50, 55	49, 51, 52, 53, 56, 58	54, 57
Six	64, 68	59, 60, 61, 62, 63, 66, 69, 70	65, 67
Seven		72, 73, 74, 76, 78, 79, 80	71, 75, 77
Eight	83, 85, 87, 89	81, 82, 84, 88	86, 87
Nine	90, 91	92, 93, 94, 95, 97, 98, 99	96
Ten	101, 105	100, 103, 104, 106, 107, 108	102, 109
Eleven		111, 112, 113, 116, 119, 120, 121	110, 114, 115, 117, 118, 122

Dictionary. Each student should have a dictionary available while doing each activity page. Moreover, it is very important that each student have a *good* dictionary. A good dictionary contains a history of word origin after each entry; it has pictures in the margins; and it has as recent a copyright date as possible, since thousands of new words enter the English language each year.

Before giving your students each worksheet, you might want to review the worksheets in a section. Which ones impress you as calling for new dictionary skills? You might want to introduce students to new dictionary skills, techniques, or even "tricks" before giving them a particular activity page. For instance, before giving students "Bird Sounds," you might want to review phonics with them briefly and show them how dictionaries use phonetic spellings. In other instances, you might prefer to show students something about the dictionary and general knowledge *after* they have done an activity page. "Horse Facts," for example, requires students to label correctly a drawing of a horse with terms such as *fetlock*, *hock*, and *mane*. Most students will look up each of the twelve words in this exercise. But in some dictionaries, the entry under *horse* contains a drawing of a horse with all of these terms labeled! So you might want to introduce students to the dictionary as a source of general knowledge after they have done the worksheet.

Master Word List. In addition to containing 122 vocabulary activity pages and an answer key, this program contains a Master Word List, organized by section, alphabetically within each section. You can use this Master Word List in several ways. You might want to hand each student a copy of the section Master Word List before you begin a section. In this way, students may at least *read* the words before they begin to think about their meanings. Introducing students to the Master Word List allows them to see the context within which they are learning a group of vocabulary words. Or you may wish to pick random words from the word list and give the students a pretest and/or a post-test for each section.

After completing the activities in *Categories*, students will have a broader understanding of the categories they studied, as well as a specific understanding of individual vocabulary words. In addition, the activities will help stretch students' general thinking skills, requiring them to make inferences, draw conclusions, and classify.

Answer Key

Section One: The Universe and the Earth

1. Terms of the Universe

1. star
2. astronomy
3. solar
4. planet
5. comet
6. constellation
7. galaxy
8. sun
9. stellar
10. meteor
11. fireball
12. nebula
13. meteorite
14. satellite
15. nova

2. From the Earth

1. terrestrial
2. almanac
3. zodiac
4. day
5. aurora
6. extraterrestrial
7. month
8. zenith
9. calendar
10. nadir

3. Space Travel

1. splashdown
2. chute
3. wing
4. fuselage
5. umbilical
6. engine
7. lunarnaut
8. stabilizer
9. earthrise
10. tank

4. Nearest Neighbor

Across

1. revolve
4. cusp
7. crater
8. tides
9. moon
10. telescope

Down

2. lunar
3. eclipse
5. rotate
6. crescent

5. The Face of the Earth

C P L A I N S B A J I H G F O M N L I K R R R Q B
N Q X A S I G J L A E B M T I H S R O S C O V Y O
G D C H O M R W C W B O T L A M A R V C O C E A N
S L I K J G U E O D N E K M V I V H S C O K R O E
C B A Z P E N I N S U L A U V W A W Y T S S R Q P
T S O K L N O H T O C J I H G F N E Y O P Y Z D H
G D G N O Q X A I S I J L T O B N W R M H C E A M
V I S L S I B N N Y B A J K T C A N Y O N A M R C
U V O X L M O E E E X D G N O F E X C H M L I W K
T S I R Q B E X N O U V E C B A Z Y P T S R U U W
D R L A K E D D T S C O N M L T I H G J E A L D O
C H O M R W E A O T L I A G M R O C P V S E I L N
B A J T K L L E D N E S A L E T V A L L E Y O B W
R M O N E I T R S T E L F A O P Y Z A C H G A D N
H F A U L T A M R W B A O C T L A M T R C V S L I
A J B I C H D G E F J N K I I C A V E L H M N G F
O K T F O R E S T S L D S E M R N Q A O P T U E V
R W Q X P Y U E V C B W A R X E Z E U D R C R O B
A S C Z D N R M O T S I C H E N M A T L I I J G H
E D F G F O N P G Q Y X Z A Y X S C A H V I H J G
L J I M O U N T A I N T I R S A B O W X E Q R M N
G H O D E C B I H L M I H S D U N E R U R C W B O

6. Bad Weather Ahead

1. T
2. T
3. F
4. T
5. F
6. F
7. F
8. F
9. F
10. F
11. T
12. T
13. T
14. T
15. T

7. More About Weather

1. climate
2. atmosphere
3. dew
4. precipitation
5. weather
6. frost
7. wind
8. season
9. front
10. humidity
11. forecast
12. mist

8. Water, Water, Everywhere

1. The **shore** is the land along the edge of the ocean—it is where the ocean (or another large body of water) touches land.
2. A **current** is a flow or movement of water within the ocean (or river).
3. A **reef** is a ridge of coral, rock, or sand that lies near the surface of the ocean (or other body of water).
4. A **tsunami** is an ocean wave caused by an earthquake. A tsunami can travel for thousands of miles and then hit a shore and do great damage.
5. A **wave** is a moving curve or ridge of water on the surface of the ocean.
6. The **ocean** is the entire body of salt water that covers the earth.
7. A **breaker** is a wave that breaks upon the shore, or that rolls over on itself.
8. A **whitecap** is a wave whose crest breaks into white foam.
9. The **littoral** is the strip of coast that is covered during high tide and exposed during low tide.
10. An **ebb tide** is the movement of the ocean away from the shore.
11. A **flood tide** is the movement of the ocean toward the shore.
12. A **lagoon** is a shallow section of ocean almost completely surrounded by land.

9. A Hot Subject

1. smoke
2. flame
3. ember
4. bonfire
5. spark
6. burn
7. blaze
8. ashes
9. kindling
10. match
11. wildfire
12. flammable

10. Misuse of the Earth

1. toxic
2. erosion
3. fallout
4. pollution
5. waste
6. sewage
7. deforestation
8. conservation
9. topsoil
10. smog

Section Two: Plants

11. Plant Parts

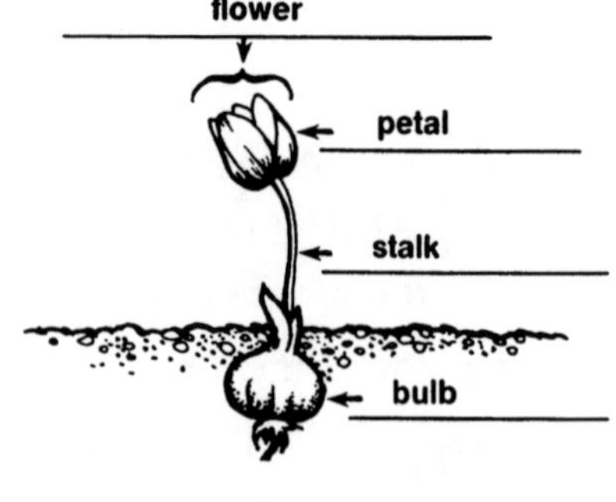

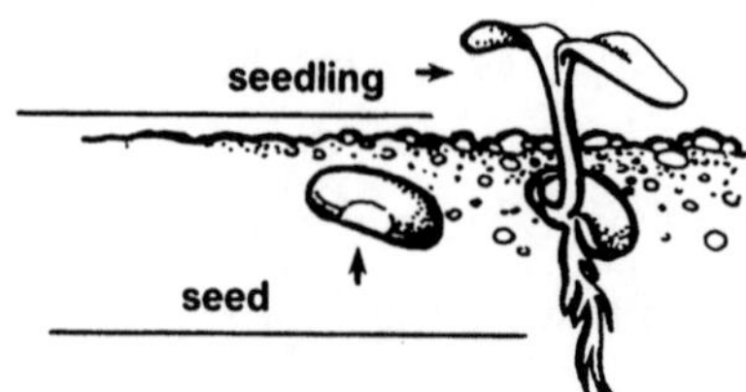

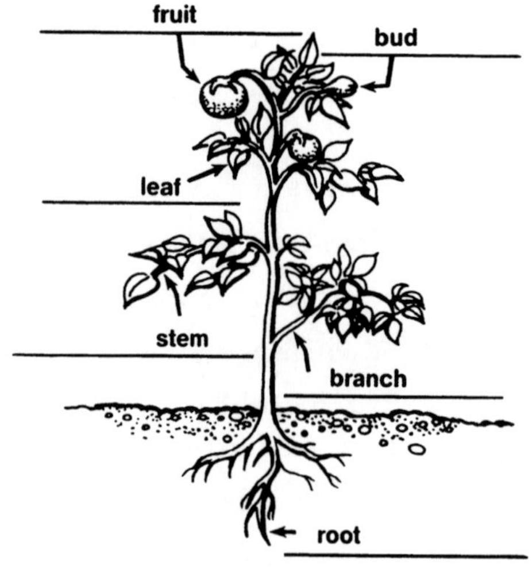

12. Rhyme Time

1. moss
2. fern
3. grass
4. fungus
5. tree
6. shrub
7. kelp
8. mold
9. plankton
10. reed

13. Words About Trees

1. d
2. h
3. c
4. k
5. a
6. j
7. l
8. i
9. b
10. g
11. e
12. f

14. Name That Tree

(Answers will vary in second part of activity.)

1. elm
2. oak
3. fir
4. ash
5. pine
6. palm
7. maple
8. beech
9. aspen
10. cedar
11. walnut
12. poplar
13. spruce
14. willow
15. pawpaw
16. buckeye
17. cypress
18. dogwood
19. hickory
20. juniper

15. Grains

Paragraph 1: grain, cereal
Paragraph 2: wheat, rice
Paragraph 3: barley, oats, rye
Paragraph 4: corn, buckwheat, sorghum

16. Bread Feast

1. pancake
2. muffin
3. bun
4. croissant
5. pita
6. bagel
7. bialy
8. tortilla
9. waffle
10. loaf
11. cracker
12. crepe

17. Circle the Fruit

1. c
2. a
3. c
4. b
5. c
6. c
7. a
8. b
9. a
10. c

18. Vegetable Truths

1. T
2. F—A crookneck is a type of squash.
3. T
4. F—A rutabaga is round, like a turnip.
5. F—A muskmelon is a cantaloupe.
6. T
7. T
8. T
9. T
10. F—Carob is the pod of a Mediterranean evergreen tree.
11. F—Almonds grow on trees.
12. T
13. F—Parsley is an herb; it is not a parsnip plant.
14. T
15. T

19. Vegetable Classification

ROOTS	LEAVES	FRUITS	STALKS/ STEMS	FLOWERS/ PODS
beet	cabbage	cucumber	asparagus	artichoke
carrot	collards	eggplant	broccoli	beans
parsnip	kale	tomato	celery	broccoli
radish	lettuce	watermelon	leek	cauliflower
turnip	spinach	zucchini	rhubarb	okra

20. Spices, Herbs, and Flavorings

1. d
2. j
3. a
4. f
5. k
6. g
7. c
8. h
9. l
10. i
11. e
12. b

21. Step Right Up

1. **Cotton** is the soft white fiber attached to the seeds of the cotton plant. It is used in making textiles.
2. **Flax** is fiber from the flax plant. It is used in making textiles.
3. **Kapok** is a silky fiber from the fruit of the silk-cotton tree. It is used as insulation or padding in clothing and life preservers.
4. **Hemp** is the fiber of the hemp plant. It is used in making ropes.
5. **Jute** is the fiber of the jute plant. It is used in making ropes and sacks.
6. **Sisal** is the fiber of the sisal plant. It is used for rope and cordage.
7. **Cork** is the light outer bark of the cork oak. It is used as a bottle stopper, in industry, and in art.
8. **Rubber** is a product made by drying the milky sap or latex of the rubber tree. It is used in electric insulation, belts, tires, and containers.
9. **Resin** is any of several sticky substances (such as copal, rosin, or amber) of plant origin used in lacquer, varnish, ink, and adhesives.
10. **Latex** is the milky, sticky sap of certain plants (such as the rubber tree) that coagulates when exposed to air. Latex is used in paints and adhesives.
11. **Turpentine** is a thin volatile oil from certain pine trees, used as paint thinner, a solvent, or in liniment.
12. **Charcoal** is a black, porous material produced by the distillation of wood, used as fuel, filters, and an absorbent.
13. **Witch hazel** is an alcoholic solution made from the leaves and bark of the witch hazel shrub. It is used externally as an astringent.
14. **Camphor** is a volatile compound obtained from the camphor tree. It is used as an insect repellent and in the manufacture of film and plastics.
15. **Penicillin** is an antibiotic compound obtained from penicillium molds. It is used to treat different diseases and infections.
16. **Digitalis** is a drug prepared from the seeds and leaves of digitalis plants. It is used as a heart stimulant.

22. Twenty Flowers

D H L O R V Y E X M A R I G O L D U
E N K G D C B B F J M O Q T W Z A T
A E I A A P P E O N Y S S I A Z H W
Z I N N I A T G Q M J E F B C G L K
N E U X S E Y O V R O L S H D A I B
C C H R Y S A N T H E M U M D E A F
G H I J K L A I M N O R N E P D Q S
T U V C A R N A T I O N F I W A X L
Y L C A Z E D C B A H G L F E F I O
J I R I S K L P H L O X O O N F M T
A L O P Q L E R S T A V W I W O Y U
E A C Z Q I S P Q T E U E R V D O S
N C U M A L A V E N D E R I J I K L
E A S B F Y C G D H L O K T U L I P
N M Q P E T U N I A A P S P T U E R

Section Three: Animals

23. Animal Homes

1. lair
2. hive
3. aerie
4. burrow
5. cave
6. den
7. warren
8. lodge
9. nest
10. cocoon

24. Fish Puzzle

Across

2. catfish
5. roe
9. gills
10. vertebrates
11. flounder
12. scavengers

Down

1. dorsal
3. scales
4. fins
6. shark
7. marine
8. spawns

25. Animal Young

1. gosling
2. kid
3. kitten
4. fawn
5. calf
6. cub
7. pup
8. leveret
9. lamb
10. foal
11. joey
12. fingerling

26. Horse Facts

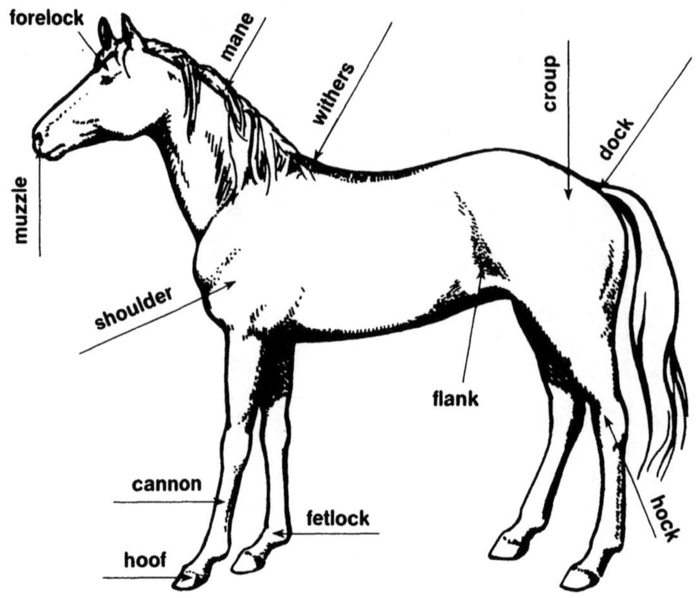

27. Reptile Word Parts

1. crocodile
2. python
3. dinosaurs
4. cobra
5. gecko
6. reptiles
7. iguana
8. turtles
9. chameleon
10. lizards

28. Which Group?

1. **Mammals** are vertebrate animals which have self-regulating body temperature, hair, and (in the female) mammary glands. *Examples:* bat, squirrel, whale
2. **Reptiles** are vertebrate animals which are cold-blooded, have lungs, have scale or plate coverings, and usually reproduce by laying eggs. *Examples:* chameleon, snake, turtle
3. **Amphibians** are vertebrate animals which are smooth-skinned, cold-blooded, and breathe through gills when young and through lungs when metamorphosed into adults. *Examples:* frog, salamander, toad

(continued)

28. Which Group? *(cont.)*

4. **Fish** are vertebrate animals which are cold-blooded, have fins, and breathe through gills. *Examples:* eel, goby, shark
5. **Birds** are vertebrate animals which are warm-blooded, have feathers and wings, and lay eggs. *Examples:* auk, owl, puffin
6. **Insects** are invertebrate animals, usually quite small. In the adult stage they have three pairs of legs and a segmented body with three major divisions. Usually they have two pairs of wings. *Examples:* ant, butterfly, wasp
7. **Arachnids** are invertebrate animals which have a hard external covering, segmented bodies, jointed limbs, and usually four pairs of legs. *Examples:* scorpion, spider, tick
8. **Mollusks** are invertebrate animals that live in water. *Examples:* mussel, octopus, snail

29. Omnivorous Words

1. e
2. i
3. a
4. l
5. j
6. g
7. f
8. h
9. c
10. k
11. d
12. b

30. Listen!

1. hoot
2. quack
3. low
4. crow
5. trumpet
6. croak
7. bleat
8. whinny
9. bray
10. coo
11. honk
12. yap
13. chirp
14. chatter
15. scream
16. chirr
17. howl
18. grunt
19. growl
20. hiss

31. Bird Sounds

1. d mockingbird
2. j jackdaw
3. g kiwi
4. e wren
5. i auk
6. a kookaburra
7. h crane
8. b toucan
9. f sandpiper
10. c quail

32. Cover-up

1. fur
2. wool
3. spines
4. skin
5. shell
6. feathers
7. scales
8. armor
9. chitin
10. hide

33. Animal Analysis

1. They are both African antelopes.
2. An **okapi** is an African mammal related to the giraffe, but smaller and with a shorter neck.
3. They are all members of the cat family.
4. A **dromedary** has one hump; a **Bactrian camel** has two humps.
5. No. **Chuckwallas** are lizards (reptiles), while **newts** are salamanders (amphibians).
6. They are all mammals.
7. A **bongo** is native to Africa, while a **guanaco** is native to South America.
8. They are all native to Australia.

34. False Colors

1. T
2. F—**Dun** is a brownish-gray color.
3. T
4. T
5. F—**Piebald** refers to an animal whose coat is spotted or patched.
6. T
7. F—**Brindled** refers to a tawny or gray animal whose coat has streaks or spots of a darker color.
8. T
9. T
10. T

35. Insect Compounds

1. A **butterfly** is an insect with a slender body, knobbed antennae, and four broad, usually colorful wings.
2. A **silverfish** is a wingless silvery-colored insect that can cause great damage to bookbindings and starched clothing.
3. A **grasshopper** is an insect with long hind legs for jumping; it can be destructive to plants.
4. A **backswimmer** is an insect that can float or swim on its back.
5. A **dragonfly** is a rather large insect that has two pairs of narrow wings and a long, slender body.
6. A **ladybug** is a small beetle usually red with black spots; it feeds on insect pests such as aphids.
7. A **glowworm** is a firefly, especially the luminous larva of a firefly.
8. A **bollworm** is the larva of a moth that is harmful to growing cotton. Bollworm also refers to the corn earworm.

36. Animal Weapons

Across

2. antlers
4. venom
5. hoofs
8. quills
10. claws
11. nails

Down

1. horns
3. teeth
6. fangs
7. tusks
9. talons

37. Creature Characteristics

1. piscine
2. feline
3. leonine
4. ophidian
5. ursine
6. vulpine
7. porcine
8. ovine
9. pachydermous
10. lupine

Section Four: The Human Body

38. Vital Organs

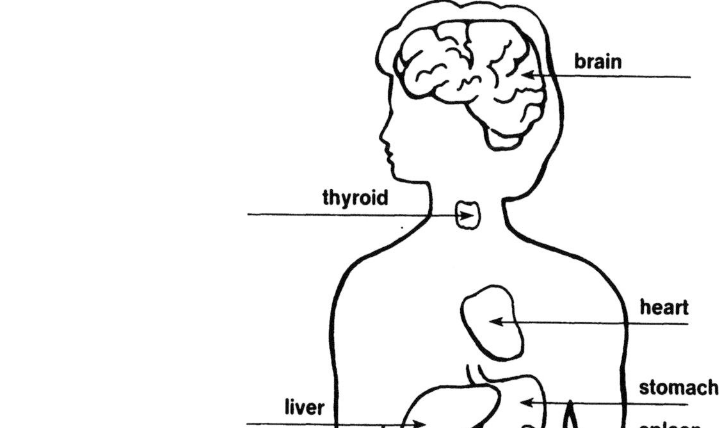

1. **organ** – a structure that performs some specific function in the body
2. **gland** – a cell or group of cells that removes selected materials from the blood and alters or eliminates these materials
3. **heart** – a hollow muscular organ that pumps blood
4. **spleen** – a ductless organ that destroys old blood cells

(continued)

38. Vital Organs *(cont.)*

5. **brain** – the part of the central nervous system that controls thought and neural coordination
6. **gallbladder** – a muscular sac in which bile from the liver is stored
7. **pancreas** – a gland that secretes digestive enzymes and insulin
8. **liver** – a large glandular organ that secretes bile and changes certain substances contained in the blood
9. **stomach** – the part of the alimentary canal that is connected to both the esophagus and the duodenum
10. **thyroid** – the large endocrine gland at the base of the neck that produces the hormone thyroxine

39. Hands Down

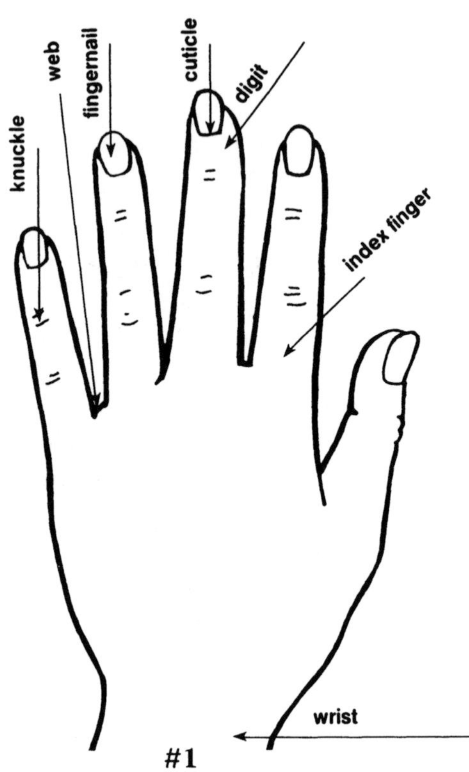

#1

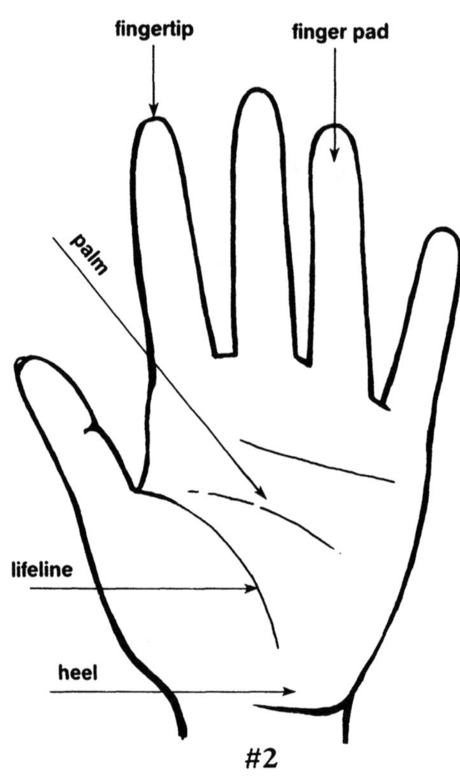

#2

40. A Real Dig

1. jawbone: mandible
2. upper-arm bone: humerus
3. wrist bones: carpals
4. breastbone: sternum
5. collarbone: clavicle
6. shoulder blade: scapula
7. hip bone: pelvis
8. tail bone: coccyx
9. thighbones: femurs
10. kneecap: patella
11. ankle bones: tarsals
12. shinbone: tibia

41. What's the System?

1. b	3. c	5. a	7. b	9. a
2. c	4. a	6. c	8. c	10. b

42. Hidden Bites

1. gum	4. pulp	7. crown	10. plaque
2. incisor	5. enamel	8. canine	11. dentin
3. cavity	6. cuspid	9. bicuspid	12. molar

43. Rhymes With

1. shock	3. abrasion	5. benign	7. bruise	9. antibiotic
2. tic	4. sterile	6. cyst	8. hernia	10. biopsy

44. Muscle Words

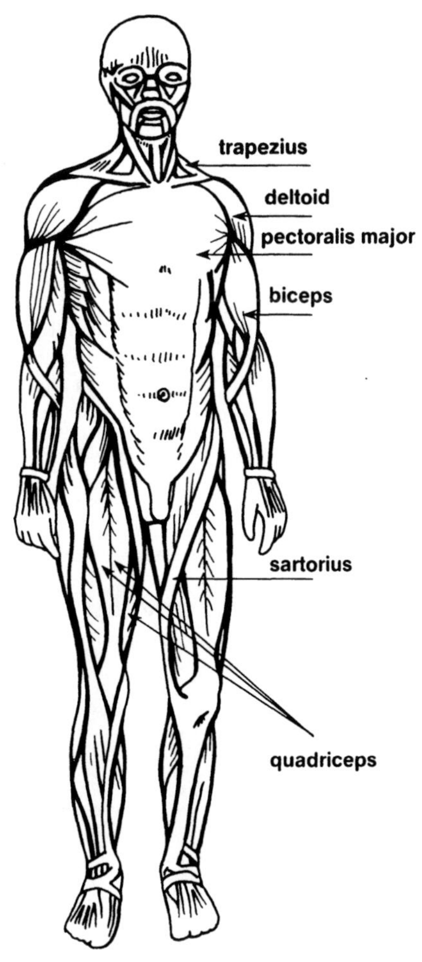

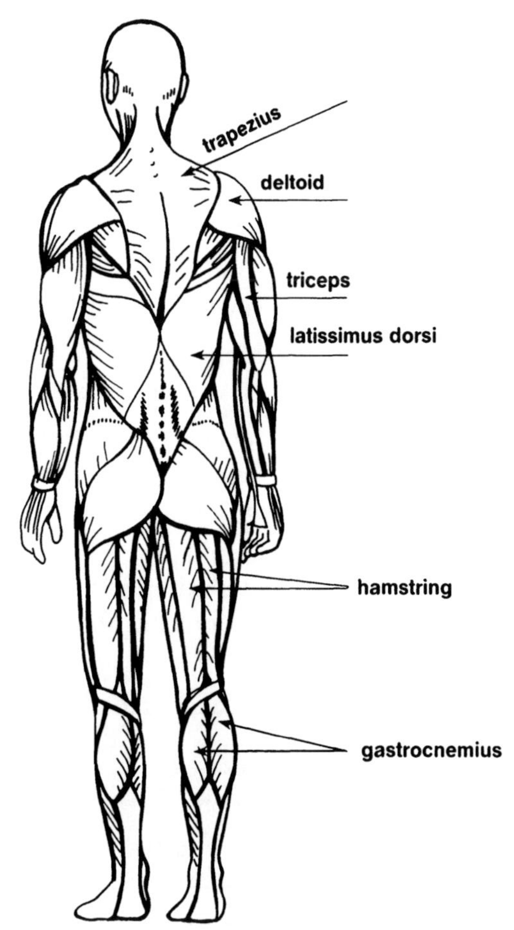

45. Body Terms

1. artery
2. esophagus
3. cartilage
4. capillaries
5. epiglottis
6. melanin
7. marrow
8. sinuses
9. lymph
10. diaphragm

46. Call the Doctor

1. neuritis
   Epilepsy is a disorder characterized by recurring attacks affecting the motor and sensory functions.
2. sty
   A **cataract** is a clouding of the eye lens; it affects vision.
3. stroke
   Shock is a loss of blood pressure and a depression of the vital processes, usually in reaction to a bodily trauma.
4. gastritis
   Colitis is an inflammation of the mucous membrane of the colon.
5. hepatitis
   Cystitis is an inflammation of the bladder.
6. lumbago
   Bursitis is an inflammation of a bursa (saclike cavity), especially of the shoulder.
7. bunion
   A **wart** is a small contagious growth on the skin caused by a virus.
8. psoriasis
   Neuralgia is pain along a nerve.
9. anemia
   Hemophilia is a hereditary disorder in which the blood does not coagulate normally.
10. tetanus
    Diphtheria is a contagious disease caused by a bacteria that attacks the mucous membrane of the throat.

47. Medical Terms Word Wheel

1. anesthetic
2. symptom
3. carcinogen
4. prosthesis
5. neurosis
6. therapeutic
7. malinger
8. intravenous
9. detoxify
10. comatose

Section Five: Houses and Other Shelters

48. Houses Around the World

1. B yurt
2. G tepee
3. A chalet
4. H igloo
5. J hogan
6. E cabin
7. C pueblo
8. K wigwam
9. L castle
10. D duplex
11. I pagoda
12. F longhouse

49. Castles on the Ground

1. f
2. j
3. l
4. b
5. a
6. g
7. d
8. k
9. h
10. c
11. i
12. e

50. Hidden Materials

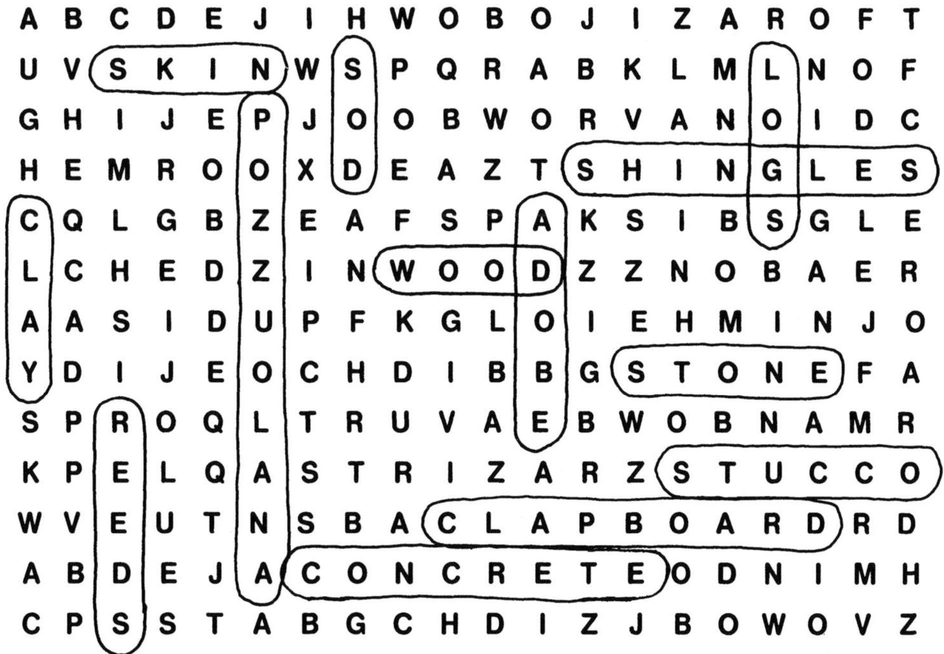

Materials from Plants: reeds, wood, logs, shingles, clapboard
Materials from Earth (Dirt): clay, adobe, sod
Materials from Animals: skin
Materials from Minerals: stone, pozzuolana, concrete, stucco

51. Stairway to Words

A **step** is a rest for the foot in ascending or descending.

Stairs are a series or flight of steps.

A **staircase** is a flight or series of steps with a supporting structure connecting different levels.

A **stairwell** is a vertical shaft around which a staircase has been built.

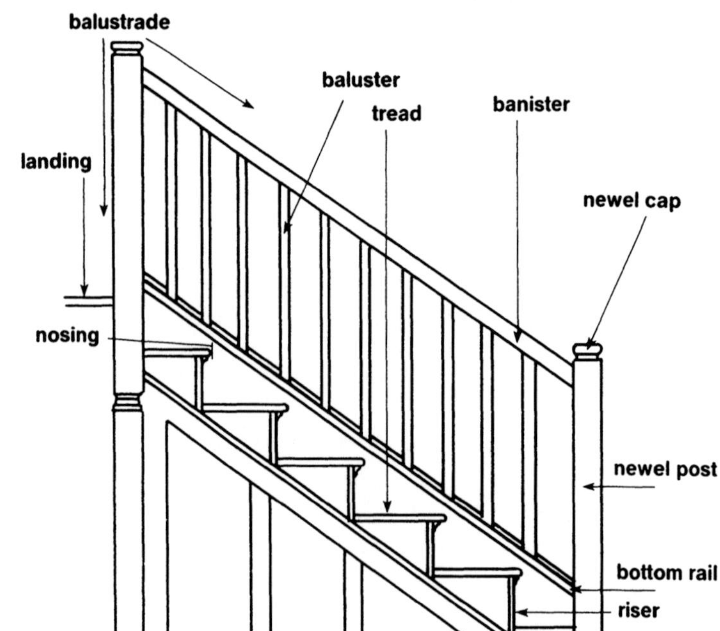

52. Houses Galore!

1. A **townhouse** (also called a row house) is a single-family dwelling of two or three stories that shares an outside wall with another such house.
2. A **condominium** is an individually owned unit (such as an apartment) in a multiunit structure (such as an apartment building).
3. A **saltbox** is a frame house with two stories in front and one story behind, with a long sloping roof.
4. A **Cape Cod cottage** is a rectangular one-story or one-and-a-half-story house that usually has a central chimney and a steep gable roof.
5. A **bungalow** is a one-story house with a low pitched roof.
6. A **ranch house** is a one-story house with a low pitched roof and an open floor plan.
7. A **split-level house** is usually a house built on three levels, with the floor level of one of the levels midway between the other two floor levels.
8. A **duplex** is a two-family house (a double house with one family living in each part). The term is also used to refer to a two-story apartment.
9. A **tenement** is an apartment house that meets minimum standards and is usually occupied by poor families in a city.
10. A **mobile home** is a trailer.
11. A **solar house** is one built to use the sun's rays to produce energy such as electricity.
12. An **A-frame** is a house with a steeply pitched gable roof that reaches to the ground on two sides. The front and rear walls of the house are thus triangular, and from the front or rear the house looks like the letter *A*.

53. Architecture Blanks

1. lintel
2. vault
3. rotunda
4. post
5. buttress
6. dome
7. column
8. apse
9. arch
10. capital

54. Household Words

1. A **window** is an opening in a wall designed to admit light or air.
   a. **casement:** a window sash that opens outward by means of hinges
   b. **sash:** a frame in which the panes of a window or door are set
   c. **sill:** the horizontal base of a window or door
   d. **skylight:** an overhead window that admits daylight
2. A **door** is a movable structure used to close an entrance.
   a. **jamb:** a vertical post or piece of a door or window frame
   b. **knob:** a rounded protuberance for grasping and opening a door
   c. **threshold:** a piece of wood or stone placed beneath a door
3. A **floor** is the surface of a room on which you stand.
   a. **linoleum:** durable, washable floor material made in sheets out of pressed linseed oil, rosin, powdered cork and pigments
   b. **parquet:** a wooden floor made of pieces of contrasting colors of wood worked into an inlaid mosaic
   c. **terrazzo:** floor material of marble or other stone chips set in mortar

55. Roof Styles

1. lean-to
2. gable
3. dome
4. mansard
5. hip
6. gambrel
7. flat
8. saltbox
9. pyramid

56. Real Estate Terms

1. interest
2. title
3. escrow
4. principal
5. appraisal
6. commission
7. earnest
8. mortgage
9. loan
10. lien

57. More Architecture

1. hall
2. atrium
3. cantilever
4. chamber
5. basilica
6. vestibule
7. belvedere
8. balcony
9. clerestory
10. courtyard
11. arcade
12. gallery

58. City Terms

1. suburb
2. skyscraper
3. inner city
4. barrio
5. gentrification
6. urbanologist
7. ghetto
8. slumlord
9. urbanization
10. rural

Section Six: Clothing

59. Clothes Crossword

Across

3. suspenders
6. knickers
7. trousers
10. slippers
13. dress

Down

1. cap
2. belt
3. shirt
4. shorts
5. skirt
8. shoes
9. blouse
11. pants
12. socks

60. Shoe Types

1. **Shoes** are outer coverings for the human foot. They are usually made of leather with a stiff sole and heel. Examples of types of shoes are: **bluchers**, **brogans**, **gillies**, **mules**, **oxfords**, **pumps**.
2. **Sandals** are shoes made of a sole that is strapped to the foot. Examples of types of sandals are: **espadrilles**, **huaraches**, **thongs**, **zoris**.
3. **Boots** are fitted coverings for the foot that usually reach above the ankle. Examples of boots are: **buskins**, **chukkas**, **jodhpurs**, **mukluks**, **Wellingtons**.
4. Examples of nonshoe leg coverings are: **puttees**, **spats**.

61. Fabric Sounds

1. b	rayon	7. i	sisal
2. j	cotton	8. d	felt
3. g	silk	9. h	nylon
4. e	ramie	10. c	raffia
5. a	wool	11. l	acrylic
6. f	linen	12. k	Orlon

62. Hats Off!

1. derby	4. cloche	7. babushka	10. sombrero
2. hood	5. beret	8. boater	11. tam
3. turban	6. fedora	9. deerstalker	12. bonnet

63. Proper Clothes

1. A **chesterfield** is a single- or double-breasted knee-length overcoat with a velvet collar.
2. **Damask** is a rich patterned cloth of silk, linen, or wool, woven to create a pattern of contrasting satiny and flat surfaces.
3. An **inverness** is a loose belted coat that has an attached cape and a round collar.
4. A **leotard** is a one-piece tight-fitting garment that covers the torso. It is worn by acrobats and dancers.
5. **Levi's** are brand-name strong cotton pants of heavy indigo-blue denim reinforced with copper rivets.
6. A **mackintosh** is a raincoat.
7. A **spencer** is a very short-waisted jacket.
8. A **trilby** is an Alpine-type soft felt hat with an indented crown.
9. A **raglan sleeve** is one that extends to the neckline, with slanted seams from the underarms to the neck.
10. A **cardigan** is a sweater that is usually collarless and that opens the full length of its center front.

64. Outer Coverings

1. anorak	4. poncho	7. Norfolk jacket	10. pullover
2. bush jacket	5. mackinaw	8. parka	11. vest
3. cape	6. cloak	9. trench coat	12. pea jacket

65. Textile Differences

1. A **thread** is a fine cord of two or more filaments twisted together. **Yarn** consists of threads twisted together in a continuous strand.
2. **Nap** is a hairy or downy surface, as on a woven fabric. **Pile** is a velvety surface produced by inserting an extra set of yarns that form raised loops which are then cut and sheared.
3. They are both coarse fibers from plants and are used in making rope and mats.
4. **Twill** is a weave of diagonal parallel ribs. **Tweed** is a rugged, nubby wool fabric made from a twill weave.
5. **Cambric** is a finely woven white linen or cotton fabric. **Poplin** is a ribbed fabric of silk, rayon, wool, or cotton.
6. **Mercerized** thread is thread that has been treated with sodium hydroxide, which shrinks it and increases its luster and color absorption.
7. **Sewing** consists of using a needle and thread to hold together pieces of fabric. **Weaving** consists of making a fabric by interlacing threads.
8. **Damask** is richly patterned. **Velvet** has a plain, dense pile.

66. Shoe Terms

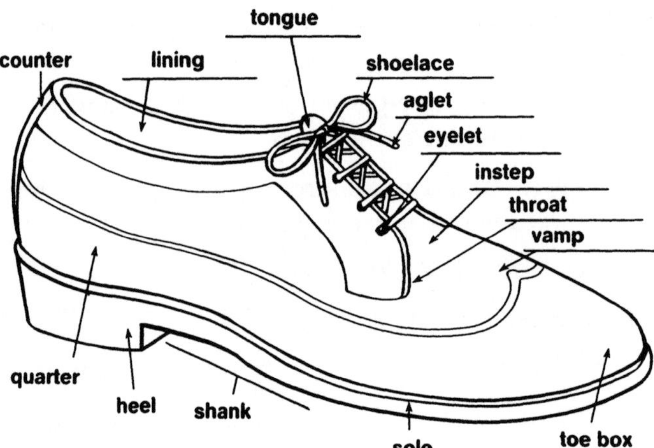

67. Clothing Museum

Paragraph 1: redingote, baldric, pelisse
Paragraph 2: jerkin/doublet, doublet/jerkin, bodice, stomacher
Paragraph 3: ruff, fichu, reticule

68. Clothes of the World

1. muu muu
2. caftan
3. bolero
4. sabot
5. kimono
6. sari
7. obi
8. dhoti
9. kilt
10. sarong
11. rebozo
12. serape

69. Fashion Words

1. mannequin
2. chic
3. trendy
4. taupe
5. mauve
6. designer
7. loden
8. couture
9. button-down
10. shirred
11. flared
12. puce
13. monogrammed
14. coordinates
15. teal

70. What Is It?

1. c
2. a
3. c
4. b
5. c
6. c
7. b
8. c
9. a
10. b
11. c
12. c
13. a
14. c
15. b

Section Seven: Transportation

71. Which Road?

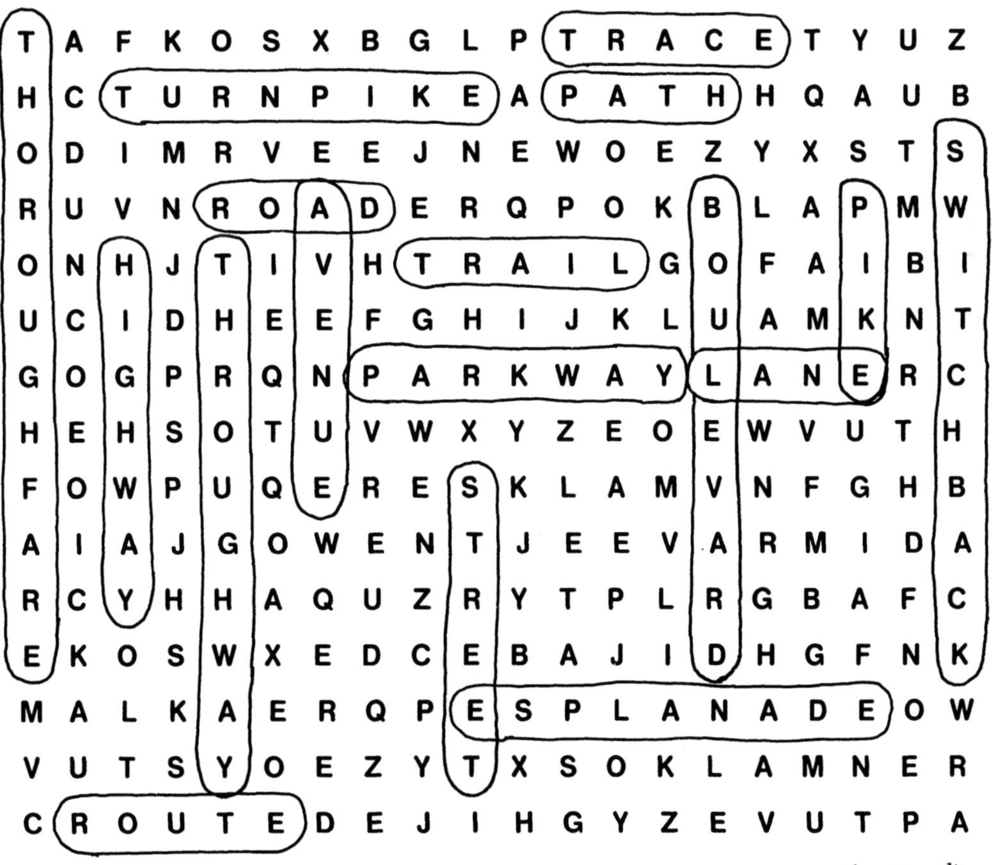

(continued)

71. Which Road? *(cont.)*

Alphabetical Order:

1. avenue
2. boulevard
3. esplanade
4. highway
5. lane
6. parkway
7. path
8. pike
9. road
10. route
11. street
12. switchback
13. thoroughfare
14. throughway
15. trace
16. trail
17. turnpike

72. Flying High

1. blimp
2. drone
3. kite
4. balloon
5. Mach number
6. drag
7. rocket
8. supersonic
9. dirigible
10. thrust

73. Anchors Aweigh

1. catamaran
2. galleon
3. dory
4. scull
5. coracle
6. skiff
7. outrigger
8. brig
9. trimaran
10. kayak
11. paddle boat
12. dugout

74. Going, Going, Gone!

1. A **coupe** is a closed, two-door automobile.
2. A **sedan** is a closed two- or four-door automobile with front and back seats.
3. A **fastback** is an automobile with a curving downward slope from the roof to the rear bumper.
4. A **hatchback** is an automobile with a sloping back containing a hatch that opens upward.
5. A **station wagon** is an automobile with an extended interior that has three rows of seats (or a luggage platform) and a tailgate.
6. A **limousine** is a large automobile driven by a chauffeur and often having a glass partition separating the passenger compartment from the driver.
7. A **van** is an enclosed truck.
8. A **pickup truck** is a light truck with an open body and low sides.
9. A **convertible** is an automobile with a top that can be folded back or removed.
10. A **dune buggy** is a small, light automobile lacking doors and a roof; it has oversized tires and a souped-up engine for driving on sand dunes.

75. What's the Word?

1. streetcar
2. bicycle
3. chariot
4. truck
5. scooter
6. bus
7. canoe
8. el
9. carriage
10. iceboat
11. train
12. rickshaw
13. skateboard
14. subway
15. submarine

76. True Sailing

1. T
2. T
3. F – A **spinnaker** is a large triangular sail that swings out opposite the mainsail; it is used on racing yachts.
4. T
5. F – **Draft** is the depth of a vessel's keel (when loaded) below the waterline.
6. T
7. F – **Leeward** refers to the side toward which the wind is blowing.
8. F – A **keelson** is a timber or girder placed above and parallel to the keel for additional strength.
9. F – The **bulwarks** are the part of a ship's sides above the upper deck.
10. T
11. F – A ship's **bow** is its front section.
12. F – **Mooring** consists of the equipment, such as anchors, for holding a vessel fast.
13. T
14. T
15. T

77. Change a Letter

(Twenty sentences will vary.)

1. tread
2. walk
3. plod
4. stride
5. strut
6. toddle
7. trudge
8. trek
9. migrate
10. stroll
11. wend
12. rove
13. prowl
14. saunter
15. roam
16. promenade
17. march
18. ramble
19. wander
20. range

78. Bicycle Wheels

1. saddle
2. pedal
3. gear
4. sprocket
5. velocipede
6. hub
7. spoke
8. bearing
9. pneumatic
10. derailleur

79. Automatic Rhyme

1. engine
2. clutch
3. starter
4. generator
5. torque
6. valve
7. carburetor
8. overdrive
9. choke
10. transmission

80. Railroad Compounds

1. roundhouse
2. highball
3. fireman
4. hotshot
5. handcar
6. crosstie
7. railroad
8. roadbed
9. telltale
10. cowcatcher
11. piggyback
12. boxcar

Section Eight: Machines and Tools

81. Kitchen Jumble

1. sieve
2. kettle
3. skewer
4. colander
5. grater
6. skillet
7. ricer
8. cleaver
9. whisk
10. blender
11. spatula
12. spoon

82. I See, I Saw

1. c
2. g
3. j
4. a
5. d
6. i
7. h
8. f
9. b
10. e

83. Computer Words

1. interface
2. printout
3. monitor
4. bit
5. memory
6. megabyte
7. binary
8. debug
9. pixel
10. initialize

84. The Sound of Weapons

1. b spear
2. f hook
3. i bolas
4. a bow
5. g sling
6. d cudgel
7. l snare
8. j boomerang
9. e net
10. h harpoon
11. c blowgun
12. k arrow

85. Name the Tool

1. adz
2. tongs
3. level
4. windlass
5. awl
6. pick
7. pliers
8. ax
9. parbuckle
10. grapple
11. chisel
12. file

86. Agricultural Tools and Machines

1. A **sickle** is a tool with a semicircular blade attached to a short handle; it is used for cutting grain and tall grasses. A **machete** is a large, heavy knife with a broad, straight blade; it is used for cutting heavy vegetation or as a weapon.
2. A **flail** is a manual threshing device consisting of a long wooden handle with a shorter, free-swinging stick attached to it. A **combine** is a power-driven harvesting machine that cuts, threshes, and cleans grain.
3. A **plow** breaks up the soil and cuts furrows. A **harrow** breaks up and evens off plowed ground.
4. A **hoe** is a hand-held tool for cultivating and weeding. A **cultivator** is a power-driven machine for doing the same thing.
5. A **windrower** is a machine that arranges cut hay or grain into long rows (called windrows) to dry in the field before being bundled.
6. **Shears** are any large instruments that cut with a scissorlike action.
7. A grain **drill** is a tool or machine for planting seeds in holes or furrows.

87. Tool Crossword

Across

1. trowel
3. broom
5. lathe
6. knife
7. lock
8. pump
9. wedge
10. plane
12. screw
16. mallet
18. hatchet
20. windmill
21. gouge
23. crane
24. boom

Down

1. tool
2. wheel
4. ramp
5. lever
9. wrench
11. nail
12. square
13. vise
14. needle
15. nut
17. bolt
19. auger
22. gib

88. Picture Perfect

1. **funnel** – a hollow cone with an extending tube, designed to catch and direct a downward flow.
2. **rolling pin** – a long cylinder for rolling out pastry dough
3. **toaster** – an electrical appliance for browning bread on both sides
4. **juicer/reamer** – an appliance for extracting juice from fruits or vegetables
5. **grater** – a tool for reducing food to small particles by rubbing
6. **baster** – a tool for moistening meat with liquid during cooking
7. **nutcracker** – a tool for cracking nuts
8. **double boiler** – two saucepans that fit together so that the contents of the upper one can be cooked or heated by boiling water in the lower one
9. **cutting board** – a board on which food is placed for cutting
10. **cookbook** – a book containing recipes and directions for cooking food

89. More Computer Words

1. modem
2. digital
3. disk
4. processor
5. chip
6. analog
7. program
8. byte
9. peripheral
10. glitch
11. software
12. nanosecond

Section Nine: Sports and Recreation

90. The National Pastime

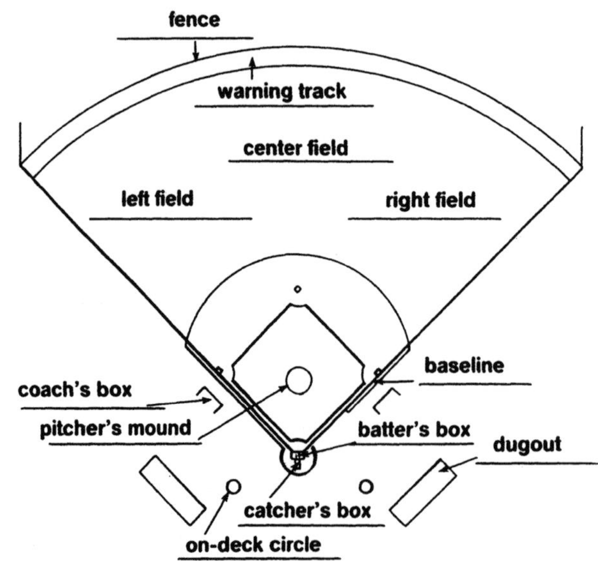

91. Which Sport?

(Twelve sentences will vary.)

1. j	4. k	7. l	10. f	13. o
2. g	5. e	8. c	11. d	14. n
3. a	6. i	9. b	12. h	15. m

92. Basketball Rhymes

1. dribble	4. basket	7. hook	10. court
2. charge	5. foul	8. drive	11. key
3. dunk	6. bank	9. feed	12. guard

93. New Sports Words

1. rabbit	4. dojo	7. schussboomer	10. orienteering
2. platoon	5. rollout	8. stuff	11. jock
3. isometrics	6. sailboard	9. turnover	12. biathlon

94. Bowling Picture

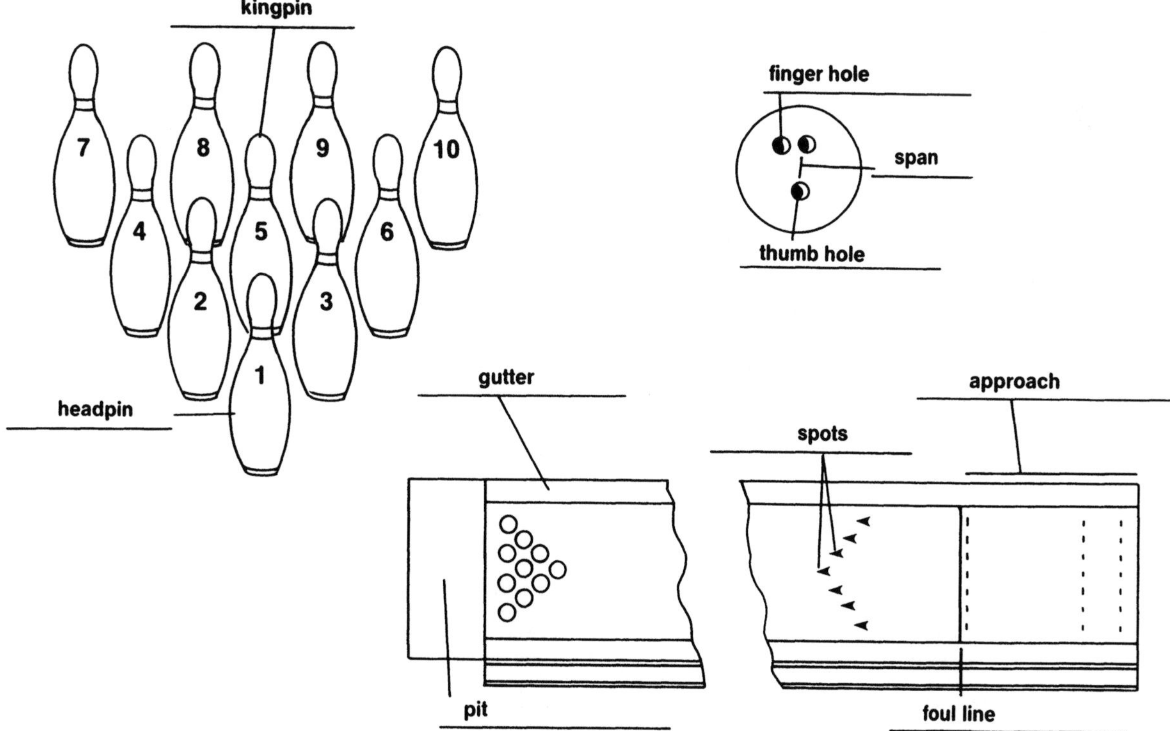

95. Sports Picture

1. D, S	4. G, Q	7. I, R	10. L, O
2. J, W	5. B, Z	8. E, Y	11. C, X
3. A, V	6. H, U	9. F, T	12. K, P

96. Twenty Sports

A B C D E J I H G F K L M N O A S R Q P T
U V W R A C Q U E T B A L L X S Y Z E R P
S K A T I N G O X A O J E D I U N D S W O
R E V R M H C B G L Q U Z Y T R P I K F L
A C B P A R A C H U T I N G C F D V E F O
G R H I G O N M L K P Q R S A I T I U V W
X O S Y Z E R O Y S T P K F A N B N G L V
Q Q Q U Z E V R M O H C D I N G S G W R O
O U U X A S O E J F E N C I N G E D C B L
A E A J I K H G F T O N M L K A S R Q P L
X T S W V I U T O B R E Z Y E K V R M H E
C B H G L I Q U B A S K E T B A L L Z R Y
W S N I D N E J O L O A X O Y Y T P K F B
A B C D E G F G H L C I J K L A M N O P A
Q R S A T U V W X Y C Z H O C K E Y E R L
B R E Z Y T U V W X E A S R Q I P K L M L
H S W I M M I N G O R J I K H N G F A B C
D E J I H F G H L M N O S E D G C B A F K
P Q R S A O N M K T E N N I S L K P T U V
H I K I N G W W E I G H T L I F T I N G R

97. Football Compounds

1. gridiron	5. halfback	9. offside
2. quarterback	6. goalpost	10. handoff
3. kickoff	7. pigskin	11. wishbone
4. touchdown	8. backfield	12. overtime

98. More Sports

1. lacrosse
2. curling
3. skittles
4. bandy
5. jai-alai
6. rugby
7. squash
8. rounders
9. spelunking
10. snooker
11. cricket
12. caber

99. Baseball Crossword

Across

4. backstop
6. baseline
8. homer
10. count
12. mound
13. runner
14. rookie
15. flake
17. pinch
18. foul
21. pitcher
22. outfield
24. steal
25. shutout

Down

1. base
2. umpire
3. balk
5. catcher
6. ball
7. strike
9. rundown
10. curve
11. doubleheader
15. forfeit
16. fly
19. shortstop
20. spike
23. double

Section Ten: Information and Entertainment

100. Words About Literature

1. c
2. b
3. c
4. c
5. a
6. b
7. a
8. b
9. c
10. b
11. a
12. c

101. The Mystery of It All

manuscript
cipher
cacography
calligraphy
paper
ink
quill
alphabet
inscription
writing

102. Give Me Music, Music, Music

1. jazz
2. rock and roll
3. rockabilly
4. gospel
5. disco
6. bluegrass
7. baroque
8. reggae
9. zydeco
10. blues
11. classical
12. swing
13. ragtime
14. folk music
15. calypso

103. Split Screen

1. program
2. network
3. anchorperson
4. noncommercial
5. docudrama
6. miniseries
7. spin-off
8. viewership
9. sanitize
10. voice-over

104. Poetry or Prose?

Poetry is metrical writing (verse) as well as writing that uses meaning, sound, and rhythm to create a specific emotional response to a subject. **Prose** is writing that has greater irregularity and variety of rhythm than does poetry and that more closely approximates everyday speech.

Poetry

1. ballad
2. canto
3. couplet
4. doggerel
5. elegy
6. haiku
7. limerick
8. ode
9. sonnet
10. stanza

Prose

antinovel
autobiography
bildungsroman
biography
epistle
essay
fable
novel
novella
roman à clef

105. Fit to Print

1. para**j**ournalism
2. edit**o**rial
3. col**u**mn
4. papa**r**azzo
5. stri**n**ger
6. fe**a**ture
7. dead**l**ine
8. synd**i**cated
9. publi**s**h
10. sa**m**izdat

	P	A	R	A	**J**	O	U	R	N	A	L	I	S	M
	E	D	I	T	**O**	R	I	A	L					
		C	O	L	**U**	M	N							
	P	A	P	A	**R**	A	Z	Z	O					
	S	T	R	I	**N**	G	E	R						
			F	E	**A**	T	U	R	E					
	D	E	A	D	**L**	I	N	E						
	S	Y	N	D	**I**	C	A	T	E	D				
P	U	B	L	I	**S**	H								
			S	A	**M**	I	Z	D	A	T				

106. The Not-So-Silent Screen

1. e dolly
2. a producer
3. h gaffer
4. b scene
5. j freeze-frame
6. d director
7. g synchronize
8. i rush
9. f documentary
10. c screen

107. Heavy Words

1. hieroglyphic
2. polyglot
3. gobbledygook
4. glyph
5. consonant
6. harangue
7. cant
8. cuneiform
9. semantics
10. trite
11. vowel
12. mellifluous

108. The Reel World

1. cinematheque
2. monochrome
3. screenplay
4. dissolve
5. projector
6. videotape
7. animation
8. feature
9. storyboard
10. cinephile
11. splice
12. dub

109. Word Fun

a. A **pun** is a play on words based on the similarity of sound between two words with different meanings.

b. A **palindrome** is a sentence that reads the same from left to right as from right to left.

c. An **oxymoron** is a figure of speech containing two terms which, taken together, seem to contradict themselves.

d. An **anagram** is a word or phrase made up by transposing the letters of another word or phrase.

e. A **neologism** is a new word, or a new meaning assigned to an old word.

f. A **nonce word** is a word invented for a particular occasion.

g. A **malapropism** is a blunder in speech caused by the substitution of one word that is similar in sound (but not meaning) to the word intended.

h. A **spoonerism** is a blunder in speech caused by transposing the initial sounds of two or more words or phrases.

i. **Litotes** is a form of understatement in which something is affirmed by expressing the negative of its contrary.

j. **Hyperbole** is extreme exaggeration.

(continued)

109. Word Fun *(cont.)*

1. c	3. f	5. e	7. a	9. j
2. d	4. b	6. h	8. g	10. i

Section Eleven: Social Institutions

110. Family Words

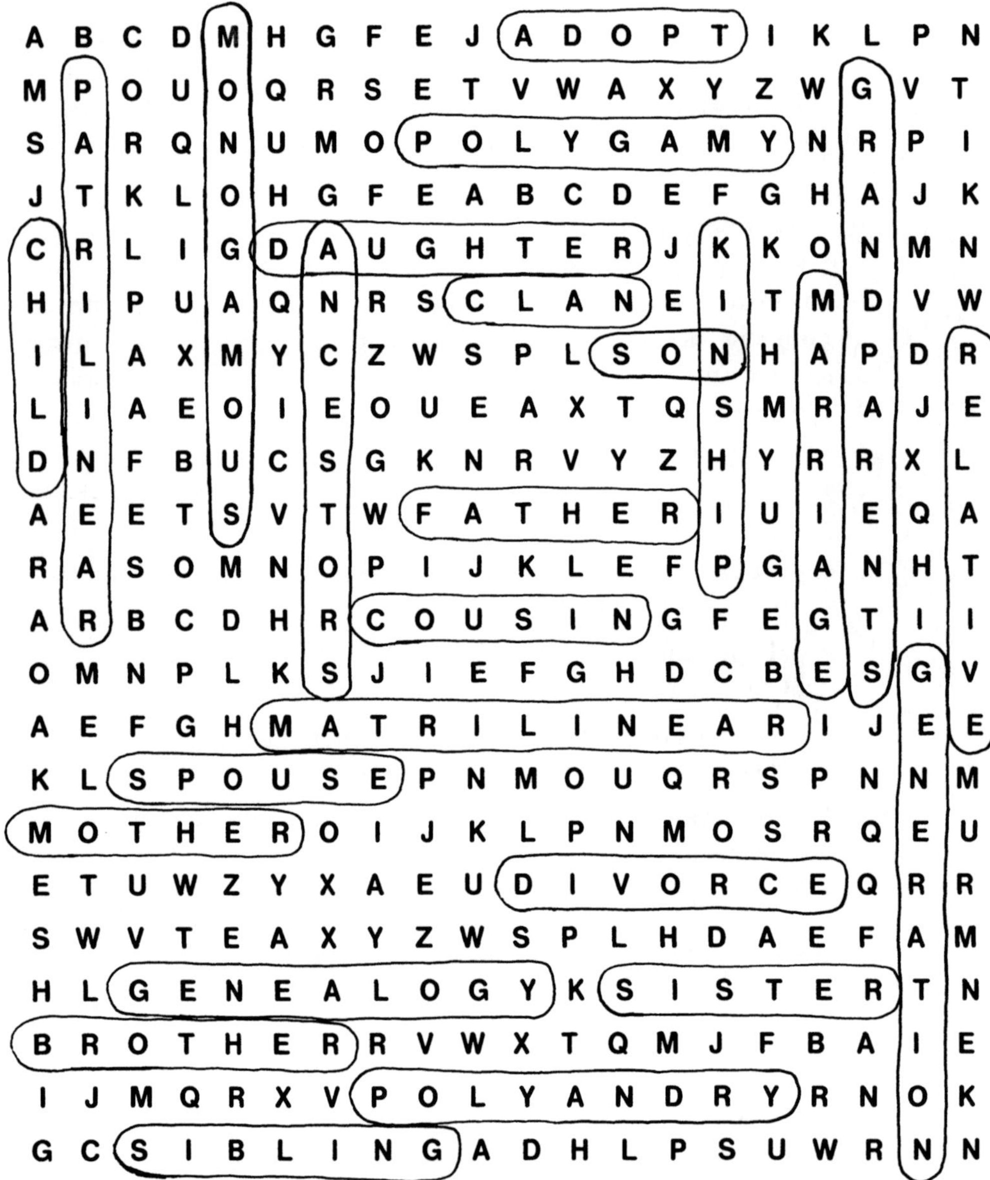

Words that apply to males only: brother, father, patrilinear, son

Words that apply to females only: daughter, matrilinear, mother, polyandry, sister

111. The Self

1. F – **Behavior** is the manner of conducting oneself, the response of an individual to her or his environment.
2. T
3. F – An **overachiever** is a person who achieves success over and above that which is expected of her or him.
4. F – **Delusion** is a persistent false belief regarding the self or objects outside the self.
5. T
6. F – **Personality** is the complex of characteristics that distinguishes an individual.
7. T
8. F – **Hallucination** is the perception of objects that have no reality, usually arising from a disorder of the nervous system or in response to drugs.
9. T
10. F – **Psychosis** is mental derangement characterized by loss of contact with reality.
11. T
12. F – An **inhibition** is an inner block to free activity or expression.

112. Legal Terms

1. acquit
2. verdict
3. deposition
4. statute
5. perjury
6. affidavit
7. sentence
8. injunction
9. arraign
10. justice

113. Work Compounds

1. burnout
2. hardhat
3. in-house
4. lowball
5. blue-collar
6. downtime
7. jury-rig
8. workload
9. flextime
10. green-carder
11. labor-intensive
12. headhunter

114. Style and Slang

1. shades
2. cutoffs
3. recycle
4. hype
5. cornrow
6. karma
7. throwaway
8. glitzy
9. trivia
10. dreadlocks

115. Educational Words

1. A **college** is a school of higher education that offers courses and grants degrees in a particular field, such as science or education. It may be an undergraduate division of a university. A **university** is a school of higher education that has graduate schools and offers M.A. and Ph.D. degrees as well as undergraduate degrees.
2. **Dyslexia** is an impairment of the ability to read; **dysgraphia** is an impairment of the ability to write.
3. (a) A **preppie** is a student in a preparatory school.
   (b) A **preppie** is a student or young adult whose manner and dress are traditional and conservative.
4. A **teacher** is one who gives instruction, usually to a large group of students. A **tutor** is a private instructor, or one who gives additional instruction.
5. **Dogmatic** means characterized by an authoritative assertion of unproved or unprovable principles.
6. A **pedant** is a person who shows off his learning; also, a pedant is a person who is unimaginative and emphasizes minute matters in teaching.
7. An **alumna** is a female graduate or former student of a school or college.
   Alumnae is the plural of *alumna*; alumnae are female graduates of a school.
   An **alumnus** is a male graduate or former student of a school.
   Alumni is the plural of *alumnus*—it refers to male graduates *and* to a mixture of male and female graduates.

116. Political Words

1. treason
2. deregulate
3. demagogue
4. schism
5. incrementalism
6. decriminalize
7. reprisal
8. coup d'état
9. imperialism
10. ombudsman
11. gerrymander
12. suffrage

117. Myth Words

1. phoenix
2. Minotaur
3. griffin
4. Valhalla
5. Excalibur
6. juggernaut
7. chimera
8. Amazons
9. Hydra
10. Atlas
11. Beowulf
12. Grendel

118. Economic Rhyme

1. tax
2. money
3. tariff
4. recession
5. inflation
6. price
7. consumer
8. trade
9. subsistence
10. depression

119. More Legal Terms

1. intestate
2. disenfranchise
3. contraband
4. battery
5. embezzle
6. extradition
7. larceny
8. manslaughter
9. codicil
10. jurisdiction
11. tribunal
12. collusion

120. Willing to Work

1. An **internist** is a specialist in internal medicine, as distinguished from a surgeon.
2. A **lapidary** is a person who cuts, polishes, or engraves precious stones.
3. A **dermatologist** is a person who treats skin, its structure, function, and diseases.
4. An **entomologist** is a person who studies insects.
5. A **farrier** is a person who shoes horses.
6. A **roustabout** is a deckhand, a longshoreman, an unskilled laborer in an oil field, or a circus worker who erects tents.
7. An **ornithologist** is a person who specializes in the study of birds.
8. A **stenographer** is a person who specializes in writing and transcribing shorthand.
9. A **cooper** is a person who makes or repairs wooden casks or tubs.
10. A **hod carrier** is a person who carries supplies to bricklayers, stonemasons, cement finishers, or plasterers on the job.
11. A **pedicurist** is a person who specializes in the treatment of the feet, toes, and nails.
12. An **etymologist** is a person who specializes in the history of words.

121. Social Issues

1. xenophobia
2. hospice
3. urbanologist
4. resegregation
5. sexism
6. environmentalist
7. underclass
8. gentrification
9. tokenism
10. slumlord

122. More Myth Words

1. d, odyssey, t
2. a, stygian, x
3. g, phobia, s
4. h, cereal, v
5. b, myrmidon, z
6. e, protean, w
7. c, martial, u
8. f, procrustean, y

Master Word List

Section One: The Universe and the Earth

almanac
ashes
astronomy
atmosphere
aurora

blaze
bonfire
breaker
burn

calendar
canyon
cave
chute
climate
cloud
comet
conservation
constellation
continent
crater
crescent
current
cusp
cyclone

day
deforestation
delta
dew
drought
dune

earthrise
ebb tide
eclipse
ember
engine
erosion
extraterrestrial

fallout
fault
fireball
flame
flammable
flood
flood tide
fog
forecast
forests
front
frost
fuselage

galaxy
gale
glacier

hail
humidity
hurricane

island

kindling

lagoon
lake
lightning
littoral
lunar
lunarnaut

match
meteor
meteorite
mist
month
moon
mountain

nadir
nebula
nova

ocean

peninsula
plains
planet
plateau
pollution
precipitation

reef
revolve
river
rocks
rotate

satellite
savanna
season
sewage
shore
sleet
smog
smoke
snow
soil
solar
spark
splashdown
stabilizer
star
stellar
storm
sun

tank
telescope
terrestrial
thunder
tides
topsoil
tornado
toxic
tsunami
typhoon

umbilical

valley

waste
wave
weather
whitecap
wildfire
wind
wing

zenith
zodiac

Section Two: Plants

allspice
almonds
apple
apricot
artichoke
ash
asparagus
aspen

bagel
banana
bark
barley
basil
beans
beech
beet
begonia
bialy
branch
broccoli
buckeye
buckwheat
bud
bulb
bun

cabbage
camphor
cantaloupe
carnation
carob
carrot
cauliflower
cedar
celery
cereal
charcoal
cherry
chrysanthemum
cinnamon
collards
conifer
cork
corn
cotton
cracker
crepe
crocus
croissant
crookneck
cucumber
cypress

daffodil
dahlia
daisy
date
deciduous
digitalis
dill
dogwood

eggplant
elm
evergreen

fennel
fern
fir
flax
flower
fruit
fungus

ginger
grain
grass

heartwood
hemp
hickory
horseradish

iris

Jerusalem artichoke
juniper
jute

kale
kapok
kelp

latex
lavender
leaf
leek
lettuce
lilac
lily
lime
loaf
lotus

maple
marigold
mold
moss
muffin
muskmelon
mustard

needle
nut
nutmeg

oak
oats
okra
orange
oregano

palm
pancake
papaya
parsley
parsnip
pawpaw
peanuts
peas
penicillin
peony
petal
petunia
phlox
pine
pineapple
pita
plankton
pomegranate
poplar

radish
reed
resin
rhubarb
rice
ring
root
rose
rubber
rutabaga
rye

sage
sap
sapwood
seed
seedling
shrub
sisal
sorghum
spinach
spruce
stalk
stem
sunflower
sweet potatoes

tomato
tortilla
tree
tree line
trunk
tulip
turnip
turpentine
twig

vegetable

waffle
walnut
watermelon
wheat
willow
witch hazel

zinnia
zucchini

Section Three: Animals

addax
aerie
amphibians
ant
antlers
arachnids
armor
auk

backswimmer
Bactrian camel
bat
birds
bleat
bollworm
bongo
bovine
bray
brindled
browse
burrow
butterfly

calf
calico
camouflage
canines
cannon
carnivorous
carrion
catfish
cave
chameleon
chatter
chirp
chirr
chitin
chuckwallas
claws
cobra
cocoon
coo
crane
croak
crocodile
croup
crow
cub
cud

dappled
den
dinosaurs
dock
dormouse
dorsal
dragonfly
dromedary
dun

eel
emu

fangs
fawn
feathers
feline
fetlock
fingerling
fins
fish
flank
flounder
foal
forelock
frog
fur

gecko
gills
glowworm
gnaw
goby
gosling
grasshopper
graze
grizzly
growl
grunt
guanaco

herbivorous
hide
hiss
hive
hock
honk
hoof
hoot
horns
howl

iguana
insects

jackdaw
joey

kid
kitten
kiwi
kookaburra

ladybug
lair
lamb
leonine
leveret
lizards
lodge
low
lupine
lynx

mammals
manatee
mane
marine
mockingbird
mollusks
mussel
muzzle

nails
nest
newts

ocelot
octopus
okapi
omnivorous
ophidian
oryx
ovine
owl

pachydermous
piebald
pinto
piscine
platypus
porcine
puffin
pup
python

quack
quail
quills

reptiles
roan
roe
root
ruminate

salamander
sandpiper
scales
scavenger
scorpion
scream
serval
shark
shell
shoulder
silverfish
skin
snail
snake
spawns
spider
spines
squirrel

talons
tapir
tawny
teeth
tick
toad
toucan
trumpet
turtle
tusks

ursine

venom
vertebrates
vulpine

warren
wasp
whale
whinny
withers
wombat
wool
wren

yap

Section Four: The Human Body

abrasion
anemia
anesthetic
antibiotic
artery

benign
biceps
bicuspid
biopsy
brain
bruise
bunion
bursitis

canine
capillaries
carcinogen
carpals
cartilage
cataract
cavity
circulatory
clavicle
coccyx
colitis
comatose
crown
cuspid
cuticle
cyst
cystitis

deltoid
dentin
detoxify
diaphragm
digestive
digit
diphtheria

enamel
endocrine
epiglottis
epilepsy
esophagus

femur
fingernail
finger pad
fingertip

gallbladder
gastritis
gastrocnemius
gland
gum

hamstring
heart
heel
hemophilia
hepatitis
hernia
humerus

incisor
index finger
intravenous

knuckle

latissimus dorsi
lifeline
liver
lumbago
lymph

malinger
mandible
marrow
melanin
molar
muscular

nervous
neuralgia
neuritis
neurosis

organ

palm
pancreas
patella
pectoralis major
pelvis
plaque
prosthesis
psoriasis
pulp

quadriceps

reproductive
respiratory

sartorius
scapula
sensory
shock
sinuses
skeletal
spleen
sterile
sternum
stomach
stroke
sty
symptom

tarsals
tetanus
therapeutic
thyroid
tibia
tic
trapezius
triceps

urinary

wart
web
wrist

Section Five: Houses and Other Shelters

adobe
A-frame
appraisal
apse
arcade
arch
atrium

bailey
balcony
baluster
balustrade
banister
barrio
basilica
belvedere
bottom rail
bungalow
buttress

cabin
cantilever
Cape Cod cottage
capital
casement
castle
chalet
chamber
clapboard
clay
clerestory
column
commission
concrete
condominium
courtyard
crypt

dome
door
duplex

earnest
escrow

flat
floor

gable
gallery
gambrel
gentrification
ghetto

hall
hip
hogan

igloo
inner city
interest

jamb

keep
knob

landing
latrine
lean-to
lien
linoleum
lintel
loan
logs
longhouse

mansard
moat
mobile home
mortgage

newel cap
newel post
nosing

pagoda
palisade
pantry
parquet
portcullis
post
postern
pozzuolana
principal
pueblo
pyramid

rampart
ranch house
reeds
riser
rotunda
rural

saltbox
sash
shingles
sill
skin
skylight
skyscraper
slumlord

sod
solar house
split-level house
staircase
stairs
stairwell
steps
stone
stucco
suburb

tenement
tepee
terrazzo
threshold
title
tower
townhouse
tread

urbanization
urbanologist

vault
vestibule

wigwam
window
wood

yurt

Section Six: Clothing

acrylic
aglet
anorak

babushka
baldric
belt
beret
blazer
blouse
bluchers
boa
boater
bodice
bolero
bonnet
boots
brogans
bush jacket
buskins
button-down

caftan
cambric
cap
cape
cardigan
cheongsam
chesterfield
chic
chukkas
cloak
cloche
coir
coordinates

cotton
counter
couture
culottes

damask
dashiki
deerstalker
derby
designer
dhoti
dirndl
doublet
dress
duck

espadrilles
eyelet

fedora
felt
fichu
flared

gillies
gusset

heel
hemp
hood
huaraches

instep
inverness

jerkin
jodhpurs

kilt
kimono
knickers

leotard
Levi's
linen
lining
loden

mackinaw
mackintosh
madras
maillot
mannequin
mantilla
mauve
mercerized
middy
monogrammed
mukluks
mules
muu muu

nap
Norfolk jacket
nylon

obi
Orlon
oxfords

pants
parka
pea jacket
pelisse

pile
pinafore
poncho
poplin
puce
pullover
pumps
puttees

quarter

raffia
raglan sleeve
ramie
rayon
rebozo
redingote
reticule
ruff

sabot
sandals
sari
sarong
serape
sewing
shank
shirred
shirt
shoelace
shoes
shorts
silk
sisal
skirt
slippers

smock
socks
sole
sombrero
spats
spencer
stomacher
suspenders

tam
taupe
teal
thongs
thread
throat
toe box
tongue
trench coat
trendy
trilby
trousers
tuque
turban
tweed
twill

vamp
velvet
vest

weaving
Wellingtons
wool

yarn

zoris

Section Seven: Transportation

astern
avenue

balloon
bearing
bicycle
blimp
boulevard
bow
boxcar
brig
bulwarks
buoy
bus

canoe
carburetor
carriage
catamaran
chariot
choke
clutch
convertible
coracle
coupe
cowcatcher
crosstie

davit
derailleur
dirigible
dory
draft
drag
drone
dugout
dune buggy

el
engine
esplanade

fastback
fireman

galleon
gear
generator

handcar
hatch
hatchback
highball
highway
hotshot
hub

iceboat

kayak
keel
keelson
kite

lane
leeward
limousine

Mach number
march
migrate
mooring

outrigger
overdrive

paddle boat
parkway
path
pedal
pickup truck
piggyback
pike
plod
pneumatic
promenade
prowl

railroad
ramble
range
rickshaw
road
roadbed
roam
rocket
roundhouse
route
rove

saddle
saunter
scooter
scull
sedan
skateboard
skiff
spinnaker
spoke
sprocket
starboard
starter
station wagon

stern
street
streetcar
stride
stroll
strut
submarine
subway
supersonic
switchback

tack
telltale
thoroughfare
throughway
thrust
toddle
torque
trace
trail
train
transmission
tread
trek
trimaran
truck
trudge
turnpike

valve
van
velocipede

walk
wander
wend

Section Eight: Machines and Tools

adz
analog
arrow
auger
awl
ax

backsaw
band saw
baster
binary
bit
blender
blowgun
bolas
bolt
boom
boomerang
bow
broom
bucksaw
byte

chip
chisel
circular saw
cleaver
colander
combine
cookbook
coping saw
crane
crosscut saw
cudgel
cultivator
cutting board

debug
digital
disk
double boiler
drill

file
flail
fretsaw
funnel

gib
glitch
gouge
grapple
grater

hacksaw
harpoon
harrow
hatchet
hoe
hook

initialize
interface

jigsaw
juicer

kettle
knife

lathe
level
lever
lock

machete
mallet
megabyte
memory
modem
monitor

nail
nanosecond
needle
net
nut
nutcracker

parbuckle
peripheral
pick
pixel
plane
pliers
plow
printout
processor
program
pump

ramp
ricer
ripsaw
rolling pin

screw
shears
sickle
sieve
skewer
skillet
sling
snare
software
spatula
spear
spoon
square

toaster
tongs
tool
trowel

vise

wedge
wheel
whisk
windlass
windmill
windrower
wrench

Section Nine: Sports and Recreation

approach
archery

backfield
backstop
balk
ball
ballooning
bandy
bank
base
baseline
basket
basketball
batter's box
biathlon
billiards

caber
catcher
catcher's box
center field
charge
coach's box
count
court
crampon
cricket
croquet
cue
curling
curve
cycling

diving
dojo
double
doubleheader
downhill ski
dribble
drive
dugout
dunk

feed
fence
fencing
figure skating
finger hole
flake
fly
forfeit
foul
foul line
Frisbee

goalpost
golf
gridiron
guard
gutter

halfback
hammer
handoff
hang gliding
headpin
hiking
hockey
homer
hook
horse
hurdle

isometrics

jai-alai
javelin
jock
jogging

karting
kayaking
key
kickoff
kingpin

lacrosse
lacrosse racket
left field

mound

offside
on-deck circle
orienteering
outfield
overtime

parachuting
pigskin
pinch
pit
pitcher
pitcher's mound
platoon
polo
puck

quarterback

rabbit
racquetball
right field
rollout
rookie
rounders
rugby
rundown
runner

sailboard
sailing
schussboomer
shortstop
shutout
shuttlecock
skating
skiing
skittles
sky diving
snooker
soccer
softball
span
spelunking
spike
spots
squash
squash racket
steal
strike
stuff
surfing
swimming

tennis
thumb hole
touchdown
turnover

umpire

volleyball

warning track
water ski
weightlifting
wishbone

Section Ten: Information and Entertainment

allusion
alphabet
anagram
anchorperson
animation
antinovel
autobiography

ballad
baroque
bildungsroman
biography
bluegrass
blues

cacography
calligraphy
calypso
cant
canto
cinematheque
cinephile
cipher
classical
column
consonant
couplet
cuneiform

deadline
denouement
director
disco
dissolve
docudrama
documentary
doggerel
dolly
dub

editorial
elegy
epistle
essay

fable
feature
folk music
freeze-frame

gaffer
genre
glyph
gobbledygook
gospel

haiku
harangue

hieroglyphic
hyperbole

ink
inscription
irony

jazz

limerick
litotes

malapropism
manuscript
mellifluous
miniseries
monochrome
motif

neologism
network
nonce word
noncommercial
novel
novella

ode
oxymoron

palindrome
paparazzo
paper
paradox
parajournalism
poetry
polyglot
potboiler
producer
program
projector
prose
protagonist
publish
pun

quill

ragtime
reggae
rockabilly
rock and roll
roman à clef
rush

samizdat
sanitize
satire

scene
screen
screenplay
semantics
simile
sonnet
spin-off
splice
spoonerism
stanza
storyboard
stringer
swing
synchronize
syndicated

theme
trite

videotape
viewership
voice-over
vowel

writing

zydeco

Section Eleven: Social Institutions

acquit
adopt
affidavit
alumna
alumnae
alumni
alumnus
Amazons
ancestors
arraign
Atlas

battery
behavior
Beowulf
blue-collar
brother
burnout

cereal
child
chimera
clan
codicil
college
collusion
consumer
contraband
cooper
cornrow
coup d'état
cousin
cutoffs

daughter
decriminalize
delusion
demagogue
demure
deposition
depression
deregulate
dermatologist
disenfranchise
divorce
dogmatic
downtown
dreadlocks
dysgraphia
dyslexia

embezzle
entomologist
environmentalist
etymologist
Excalibur
extradition

farrier
father
flextime
flippant

genealogy
generation
gentrification
gerrymander
glitzy
grandparents
green-carder
Grendel
griffin

hallucination
hardhat
headhunter
hod carrier
hospice
Hydra
hype

imperialism
incrementalism
inflation
inhibition
in-house
injunction
internist
intestate

juggernaut
jurisdiction
jury-rig
justice

karma
kinship

labor-intensive
lapidary
larceny
lowball

mania
manslaughter
marriage
martial
matrilinear
Minotaur
money
monogamous
mother
myrmidon

odyssey
ombudsman
ornithologist
overachiever

patrilinear
pedant
pedicurist
perjury
personality
phobia
phoenix
polyandry
polygamy
preppie
price
procrustean
protean
psychosis

recession
recycle
relative
reprisal
resegregation
roustabout

schism
self-actualize
sentence
sexism
shades
sibling
sister
slumlord
son
spouse
statute
stenographer
stygian
sublimation
subsistence
suffrage

tariff
tax
teacher
throwaway
tokenism
trade
treason
tribunal
trivia
tutor

underclass
university
urbanologist

Valhalla
verdict

workload

xenophobia

Index to All Words

Number(s) indicate on which master(s) the word is used.

Name ______________________________ Date ______________

Terms of the Universe

Astronomy, comet, constellation, fireball, galaxy, meteor, meteorite, nebula, nova, planet, satellite, star, stellar, solar, sun – these words are hidden below, one in each row. Read each clue, then circle the one word in each row that goes with the clue. You may look up words in your dictionary.

Clue	Letters
1. body in space that shines, gives off its own light	S K A L E S T A R N E V O C A T A S R M
2. study of stars and other things in space	A B R A S T R O N O M Y P I T I O N R S
3. having to do with the sun	B L A R I G R A S T O S O L A R I N I G
4. body in space; does not give off light	E A R M I E A R P I P L A N E T M N O N
5. orbits the sun; may have tail	N O C O M E T R A I P A R N C S H O M E
6. pattern in sky made by certain stars	P A T C R O M C O N S T E L L A T I O N
7. vast, gigantic system of stars	A S T O I D G A L A X Y S O L I P I N G
8. the star closest to us	M E R C U R V E S U N N I N O V R O M E
9. having to do with a star or stars	S T E L L A R S T A I S O C R A B R O T
10. fragment traveling through space	C R O M M W E M E T E O R A M S B I C K
11. very large meteor that burns in the sky	F R E P H O P H U M F I R E B A L L O R
12. immense body of gas or dust in space	S K O S K N I N E B U L A M I N T R O X
13. a meteor that has hit the ground	D U S E N M E T E O R I T E X C A C H S
14. a body that orbits a larger body	H E A V A S T R A S A T E L L I T E C H
15. a star that bursts into brilliance	S U P A C L U S E N O V A R I N G E O R

Characters of the Universe On the back of this sheet of paper, list all the fictional characters you can think of who come from another planet. The characters may be from books, comic books, or films.

Name ______________________________ Date ______________

From the Earth

Fill in the blanks below by writing the correct word on each line. You may use your dictionary.

day	**aurora**	**zenith**	**terrestrial**	**zodiac**
month	**nadir**	**almanac**	**extraterrestrial**	**calendar**

1. Anything that is from the earth or has to do with the earth is ______________________ .
2. A(n) ______________________ is a book of information about sunrise, sunset, moon phases, tides, and other such things.
3. The ______________________ is an imaginary belt around the sky which is divided into twelve constellations.
4. A(n) ______________________ is the time it takes the earth to rotate once on its axis.
5. The glow of lights in the far northern and far southern skies, the ______________________ , is colorful and beautiful.
6. Anything that comes from outside the earth (that is, from space) is ______________________ .
7. A(n) ______________________ is the time it takes the moon to circle the earth once.
8. The ______________________ is a point in the sky directly above your head; the word also means "highest point."
9. A system for arranging time (days, weeks, months) into order is a(n) ______________________ .
10. The ______________________ is a point in the sky on the other side of the earth, directly below your feet; the word also means "lowest point."

Earth, Earth, Earth Look up the word ***terrestrial***. On the back of this sheet of paper, write the Latin root that it comes from. Then use your dictionary to find at least five other words that come from the same root. List the words and write their definitions.

Name ______________________________ Date ____________

Space Travel

Study the vocabulary words, then study the pictures. Write the word that best describes or explains each picture on the line next to it. You may use your dictionary.

tank	fuselage	splashdown	earthrise	engine
wing	umbilical	lunarnaut	stabilizer	chute

1. ______________________
2. ______________________
3. ______________________
4. ______________________
5. ______________________
6. ______________________
7. ______________________
8. ______________________
9. ______________________
10. ______________________

Space-Age Compound Words Words such as ***splashdown*** and ***earthrise*** are new words. They are also compound words. A compound word is one word made out of two other words (*splash* + *down* = *splashdown*). On a separate sheet of paper, write a science fiction story in which you use five new compound words that you make up yourself. After the story, write a definition of each of your five new compound words.

Name ______________________________ Date ______________

Nearest Neighbor

Solve the crossword puzzle by writing the correct word in each blank. You may use a dictionary.

Across

1. to travel in a circle or orbit
4. the pointed end, or horn, of a crescent moon
7. a bowl-shaped cavity on the surface of the moon
8. the risings and fallings of the ocean waters caused by the gravitational pull of the moon
9. Earth's nearest neighbor in space
10. an instrument that makes distant objects appear larger and nearer

Down

2. having to do with the moon
3. the total hiding of the sun by the moon
5. to turn around a center point such as an axis
6. the shape of the moon in its first or last quarter

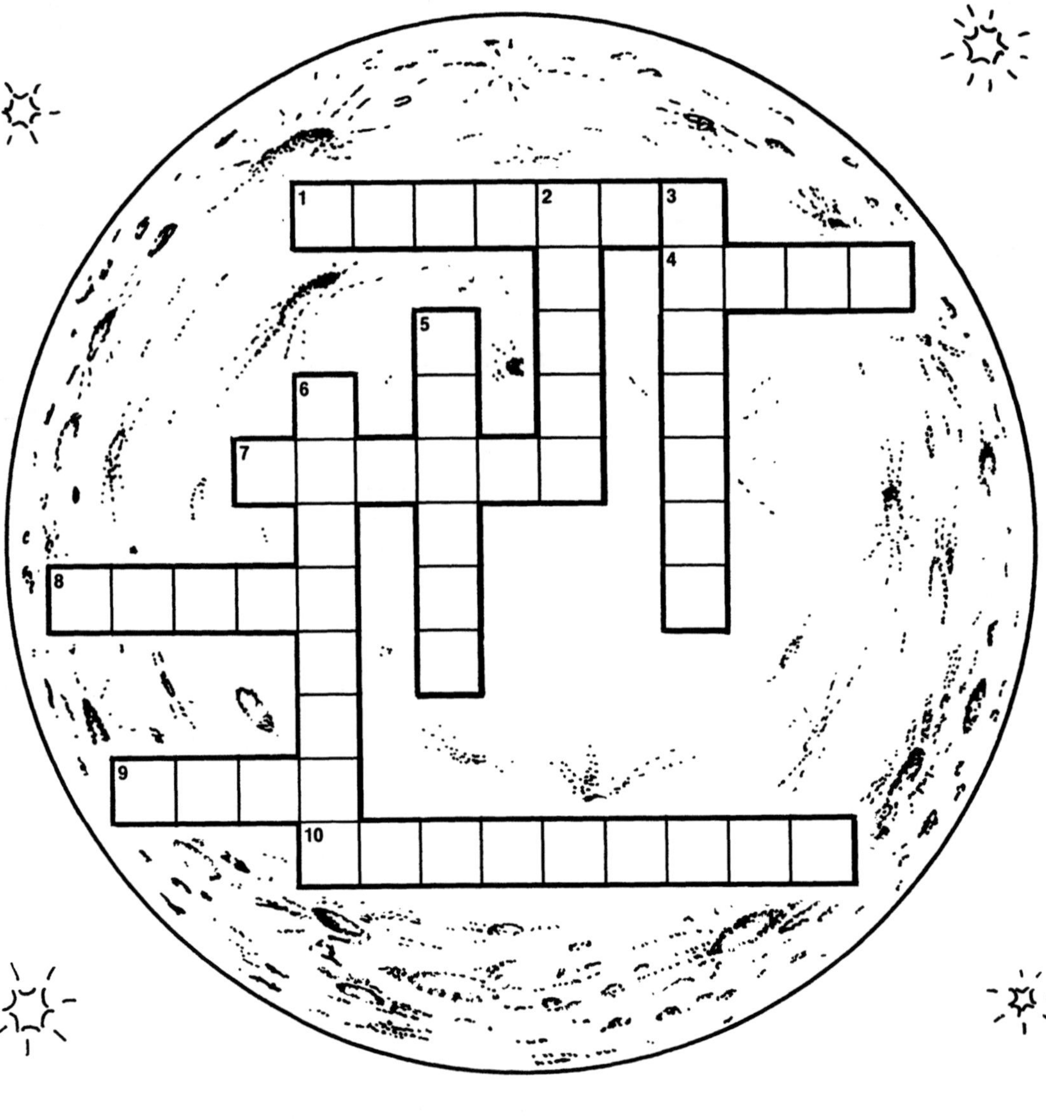

Lunar Fiction The French novelist Jules Verne (1828–1905) is considered the originator of modern science fiction. Read his novel, *From the Earth to the Moon*, and write a report on its plot and theme.

Name ______________________________ Date ______________

The Face of the Earth

Hidden in the letters below are twenty words that name some feature on the face of the earth. The words run from left to right or from top to bottom. Circle each of the twenty words. You may use a dictionary. The following paragraph uses all twenty words; many words that are plural in the paragraph are singular in the puzzle.

The earth's face has many physical features. Mapmakers see land as **continents**, **islands**, and **peninsulas**. Hikers see **mountains** and **valleys**, **plateaus** and **canyons**. Farmers see **soil**, **plains** and **savannas**, and **forests**. Sailors know that there is one **ocean**, which goes by many names. Long ago pioneers looked for vital water sources: **rivers** (some with **deltas**) and **lakes**. Beachgoers like **dunes**. Purists are fascinated by **glaciers**. Geologists study **rocks**, speleologists explore **caves**, and earthquake experts worry about **faults**.

```
C P L A I N S B A J I H G F O M N L I K R R R Q B
N Q X A S I G J L A E B M T I H S R O S C O V Y O
G D C H O M R W C W B O T L A M A R V C O C E A N
S L I K J G U E O D N E K M V I V H S C O K R O E
C B A Z P E N I N S U L A U V W A W Y T S S R Q P
T S O K L N O H T O C J I H G F N E Y O P Y Z D H
G D G N O Q X A I S I J L T O B N W R M H C E A M
V I S L S I B N N Y B A J K T C A N Y O N A M R C
U V O X L M O E E E X D G N O F E X C H M L I W K
T S I R Q B E X N O U V E C B A Z Y P T S R U U W
D R L A K E D D T S C O N M L T I H G J E A L D O
C H O M R W E A O T L I A G M R O C P V S E I L N
B A J T K L L E D N E S A L E T V A L L E Y O B W
R M O N E I T R S T E L F A O P Y Z A C H G A D N
H F A U L T A M R W B A O C T L A M T R C V S L I
A J B I C H D G E F J N K I I C A V E L H M N G F
O K T F O R E S T S L D S E M R N Q A O P T U E V
R W Q X P Y U E V C B W A R X E Z E U D R C R O B
A S C Z D N R M O T S I C H E N M A T L I I J G H
E D F G F O N P G Q Y X Z A Y X S C A H V I H J G
L J I M O U N T A I N T I R S A B O W X E Q R M N
G H O D E C B I H L M I H S D U N E R U R C W B O
```

Dictionary Features On the back of this sheet of paper, list ten of the twenty words you circled. Write a dictionary definition for each of the ten words.

Name ________________________________ Date ________________

Bad Weather Ahead

Read each sentence below and think about the definition of the boldfaced word. Circle **T** if a statement is true. Circle **F** if it is false. You may use a dictionary.

T F 1. A **cloud** is visible fog in the sky.

T F 2. **Snow** is precipitation in the form of small ice crystals.

T F 3. **Thunder** is the sound before lightning is discharged.

T F 4. A **cyclone** is a storm whose winds rotate around a center.

T F 5. **Hail** is partially frozen rain.

T F 6. A period of excessive rain is called a **drought**.

T F 7. A cyclone at sea is a **tornado**.

T F 8. A **gale** is a wind lighter than a breeze.

T F 9. **Sleet** is precipitation in the form of small lumps of ice.

T F 10. A cyclone on land is called a **hurricane**.

T F 11. A **typhoon** is a tropical cyclone.

T F 12. A disturbance of the atmosphere that results in wind and rain, snow, hail, sleet, thunder, or lightning is a **storm**.

T F 13. A **flood** is the rising and overflowing of a body of water onto dry land.

T F 14. The discharge of electricity in the atmosphere is called **lightning**.

T F 15. A **fog** consists of water vapor suspended in the air close to the ground.

Weather Experience On a separate sheet of paper, write three paragraphs on your most memorable experience with the weather.

Name ______________________________ Date ______________

More About Weather

Read each definition below. Circle the one word that matches each definition. You may use a dictionary.

1. the usual weather of a place	**temperature**	**climate**	**seasons**
2. the air surrounding the earth	**atmosphere**	**humidity**	**front**
3. small droplets of condensed air moisture	**showers**	**dew**	**frost**
4. the falling of rain, snow, sleet, hail or mist	**precipitation**	**humidity**	**rain**
5. the condition of the atmosphere	**evaporation**	**humidity**	**weather**
6. frozen dew	**precipitation**	**frost**	**front**
7. the movement of the air	**weather**	**frost**	**wind**
8. a period of time that has a certain kind of weather	**atmosphere**	**season**	**front**
9. boundary between two unlike air masses	**barometer**	**forecast**	**front**
10. amount of dampness in the air	**precipitation**	**humidity**	**frost**
11. to predict the weather	**monsoon**	**forecast**	**alter**
12. falling water whose droplets are finer than rain	**monsoon**	**front**	**mist**

Weather Picture On a separate sheet of paper, draw a picture that illustrates at least four of the words you have circled above. Label the parts of the drawing that illustrate the words you have chosen.

Name ______________________________ Date ______________

Water, Water, Everywhere

All the words below are about the ocean. Look up each word in a dictionary. Write a definition of each word.

1. **shore** ______________________________

____

2. **current** ______________________________

____

3. **reef** ______________________________

____

4. **tsunami** ______________________________

____

5. **wave** ______________________________

____

6. **ocean** ______________________________

____

7. **breaker** ______________________________

____

8. **whitecap** ______________________________

____

9. **littoral** ______________________________

____

10. **ebb tide** ______________________________

____

11. **flood tide** ______________________________

____

12. **lagoon** ______________________________

____

Soggy Story On a separate sheet of paper, write a humorous story entitled "Never Leave Your Beach Towel on the Littoral."

Name ______________________ Date ______________

A Hot Subject

Ashes, blaze, bonfire, burn, ember, flame, flammable, kindling, match, smoke, spark, wildfire – these words are scrambled below. Unscramble each word and write it on the line next to its brief definition. You may use a dictionary.

kosem	____________	1. visible particles of carbon suspended in vapor
lafme	____________	2. a single light of fire that is tongue-shaped
berem	____________	3. a glowing piece of wood or coal
froebin	____________	4. a large fire that is built outdoors
praks	____________	5. a tiny glowing bit of burning matter
rubn	____________	6. to set on fire; to destroy by fire
zebal	____________	7. a fire that is burning strongly
hases	____________	8. the gray powder that is the remains of burnt matter
linnkgid	____________	9. bits of easily lighted materials to start a fire
thamc	____________	10. small piece of wood treated to catch fire by friction
flewridi	____________	11. a very destructive, rapidly spreading fire
labmelfam	____________	12. easily set on fire

Hot Research Use the library to research the subject of fire. Read about the ways that different groups of early people made fire. Write a two-page report on three early ways to make fire.

Name ______________________________ Date ______________

Misuse of the Earth

p o l l u t i o n s m o g t o x i c d e f o r e s t a t i o n w a s t e

There are ten words in the letters at the top and bottom of this page. Separate the letters into words; then write the correct word on each line below. You may use a dictionary.

1. Something that is poisonous is ______________________ .
2. ______________________ is the wearing away of land.
3. ______________________ refers to radioactive particles in the atmosphere.
4. The act of making the earth impure, unclean, or contaminated is called ______________________ .
5. The unwanted products and byproducts manufactured by human beings are called ______________________ .
6. ______________________ is human waste matter carried off by sewers.
7. Removing forests from the land is called ______________________ .
8. ______________________ is the planned protection and management of the natural environment.
9. The fragile, easily destroyed surface soil in which plants grow is ______________________ .
10. ______________________ is a fog made heavy and dark by the mixing of smoke and chemical fumes with regular water vapor.

e r o s i o n t o p s o i l s e w a g e f a l l o u t c o n s e r v a t i o n

Council Speech Imagine that you have been elected to your town's council as a representative of your neighborhood. The council is debating pollution. What do you have to say on the subject? On a separate sheet of paper, outline a speech on the subject. Your outline should contain at least two main heads and at least two subheads under each main head.

Name ______________________________ Date ______________

Plant Parts

Study the three diagrams below. Write the correct vocabulary word on each line of the diagrams. You may use the dictionary.

bud	**bulb**	**seed**	**petal**	**stalk**	**branch**
fruit	**stem**	**root**	**seedling**	**flower**	**leaf**

Double Duty Many of the twelve words above have more than one meaning. ***Stalk***, for example, is not only a noun that names a part of a plant, but also a verb with a completely different meaning. On the back of this sheet of paper, write the word ***stalk*** and, next to it, write one of its nonplant definitions. Then do the same for four other words from the list.

Name ______________________________ Date ______________

Rhyme Time

Read each definition below. Write the answer on the line. The answer rhymes with the boldfaced word or words. (Remember that words that rhyme are not always spelled similarly.) You may use the dictionary.

1. This is a small green plant.

   Will the **boss toss** the ______________ at **Ross**?

2. This is a flowerless, seedless plant with graceful fronds.

   When will you **learn** to **turn** the ______________?

3. This plant has narrow leaves and hollow stems.

   I will **pass** on raking the **mass** of ______________.

4. This entire plant group lacks chlorophyll. The group includes yeast, mold, smut, and mushroom plants.
   Farley wrote a story about a **humongous** ______________ that grew on the football field.

5. A tall, woody plant, it has a single trunk.

   Gee, we had to pay a **fee** to view the ______________.

6. A woody plant of somewhat low height, it has several stems.

   Don't **flub** when you plant the ______________ in the **tub**.

7. This is brown seaweed, usually very large.

   I will **yelp** for **help** if attacked by ______________.

8. This is a fungus that causes disintegration of organic matter.

   You can't get me to **hold** that ______________.

9. This collection of tiny plant and animal organisms that drift in the water provides food for whales.
   His idea of **Yank fun** is hunting for ______________.

10. This is a particular type of tall grass.

    Weed the **weed**, not the ______________.

Plant Rant On a separate sheet of paper, write a poem using at least five of the answer words from this page.

Name ______________________________ Date ____________

Words About Trees

Write the letter of the correct answer next to each brief definition. You may use a dictionary.

______	1. losing all leaves at some time during the year	a. **twig**
______	2. the main stem of a tree	b. **bark**
______	3. the older, darker, harder wood at the center of a tree trunk	c. **heartwood**
______	4. a visible circle of growth in a cross-section of a tree trunk	d. **deciduous**
______	5. a small branch that supports buds, leaves, flowers, and seeds	e. **needle**
______	6. the newer, lighter, softer wood at the outer edge of a tree trunk	f. **sap**
______	7. the limit in latitude or altitude beyond which trees do not grow	g. **conifer**
______	8. keeping leaves at all times of the year	h. **trunk**
______	9. outer, waterproof covering of a tree	i. **evergreen**
______	10. a cone-bearing evergreen such as hemlock, spruce, or fir	j. **sapwood**
______	11. a stiff, narrow leaf	k. **ring**
______	12. the liquid in a tree (or other plant)	l. **tree line**

Tree List On a separate sheet of paper, write the letters of the alphabet from A to Z. Next to each letter, write the name of a tree that begins with that letter. How close to twenty-six can you get?

Name ______________________________ Date ______________

Name That Tree

Each word on the left-hand side of the page *almost* names a type of tree. Only one letter is wrong in each word. Change the wrong letter to a correct letter and write the name of the tree in the center column. Then, in the space on the right, write a brief piece of information about the tree—you will find information in the dictionary. (For example, next to **oak**, you might write: "Acorns grow on oaks.") In order to complete this exercise, you may work with a partner. You may use a dictionary.

1. alm _ _ _ ______________
2. tak _ _ _ ______________
3. far _ _ _ ______________
4. ask _ _ _ ______________
5. pint _ _ _ _ ______________
6. calm _ _ _ _ ______________
7. maile _ _ _ _ _ ______________
8. leech _ _ _ _ _ ______________
9. ashen _ _ _ _ _ ______________
10. dedar _ _ _ _ _ ______________
11. warnut _ _ _ _ _ _ ______________
12. toplar _ _ _ _ _ _ ______________
13. spouce _ _ _ _ _ _ ______________
14. billow _ _ _ _ _ _ ______________
15. pappaw _ _ _ _ _ _ ______________
16. busheye _ _ _ _ _ _ _ ______________
17. capress _ _ _ _ _ _ _ ______________
18. dogword _ _ _ _ _ _ _ ______________
19. hicrory _ _ _ _ _ _ _ ______________
20. junifer _ _ _ _ _ _ _ ______________

What's the Difference? Look up any three trees in an encyclopedia. Then, on a separate sheet of paper, write a description of how the three trees differ from one another. Explain how to recognize each of the trees.

Name ______________________________ Date ______________

Grains

Read the essay below. Fill in each blank with the correct vocabulary word. You may use the dictionary and, if necessary, an encyclopedia. (Two of the words below do not belong in the essay.)

barley	**buckwheat**	**rice**	**groats**	**corn**	**grain**
oats	**couscous**	**rye**	**cereal**	**sorghum**	**wheat**

The most important food source in the world is ________________, which is simply a small, hard seed or fruit produced by a certain type of grass plant. These grass plants are called the ________________ grasses. (The word comes to us from the Roman goddess Ceres, the goddess of grain.)

________________ is the most common and most important grain in the western world. Most of our bread is made from it. So are our waffles, pancakes, muffins, and other types of bread. So are pasta products. In the eastern world, ________________ is the most important grain. It is eaten directly as a grain, seldom made into bread or anything else. It is easy to cook by boiling or steaming.

One of the oldest of cultivated grains is ________________, which today is used mainly in brewing beer and ale. When eaten, it is often used in soups, particularly hearty soups such as Scotch broth. Another hearty grain that many people associate with Scotland, where it is a principal crop, is ________________. Although this grain is mainly fed to animals, humans eat it as a breakfast cereal: the rolled grains are cooked in water. Still another hearty grain is ________________, which is used in making pumpernickel bread and in blending a certain kind of whiskey.

The grain that Americans call ________________ is also called maize. It is a New World crop taken back to Europe by the early explorers of North and South America. ________________, on the other hand, is native to central Asia. It is used in soups and porridge, but is technically not a grain, even though it is eaten as one. In the New World, it is often added to pancake batter to flavor the pancakes. Last of all, there is ________________, which looks something like corn but is native to the Old World. In the New World it is used mainly to make a sweet syrup or as cattle feed, but in the Old World it is a food staple.

Grain Crisis Imagine a crisis of some sort that suddenly threatens all the grains in the world. On a separate sheet of paper, list ten possible results of a worldwide grain crisis.

Name ______________________________ Date ______________

Bread Feast

Study the pictures of various types of breads. Write the correct word next to each picture by filling in the missing letters. You may use your dictionary.

1. _ _ n _ _ k _

2. m _ _ _ i _

3. _ _ n

4. _ r _ _ s _ _ _ _ _

5. _ _ t _

6. _ _ g _ _

7. b _ _ l _

8. _ o _ _ _ _ _ _ a

9. _ _ _ f l _

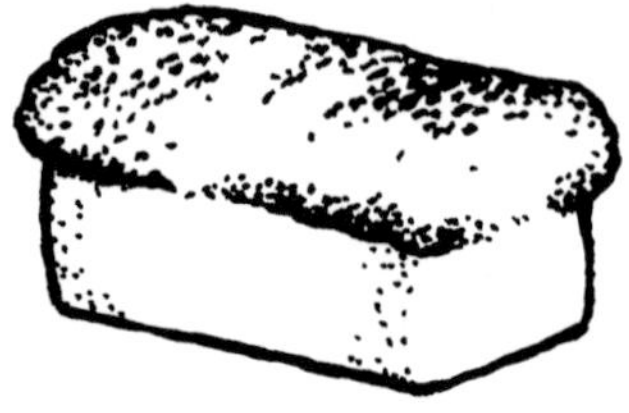

10. _ _ _ f

11. _ _ a _ k _ _

12. _ _ _ p e

Imagine Bread Imagine that you must describe bread to somebody who has never seen, smelled, or tasted it. Write a one-page description of bread.

Name ______________________________ Date ______________

Circle the Fruit

Read each definition below. Write the letter of the correct fruit on each line. You will need a dictionary in order to check descriptions and definitions.

______ 1. An oval, orange-colored fruit, *Prunus armeniaca*

(a) **peach** (b) **plum** (c) **apricot**

______ 2. Genus *Prunus*, fruit can be yellow, red, or black, smooth and round, contains a smooth seed

(a) **cherry** (b) **mango** (c) **fig**

______ 3. Fruit has reddish-yellow rind, sweet pulp, genus *Citrus*

(a) **pineapple** (b) **lime** (c) **orange**

______ 4. Genus *Carica*, tropical American fruit, oblong and yellow

(a) **banana** (b) **papaya** (c) **pomegranate**

______ 5. A round pome fruit, red or yellow, genus *Malus*

(a) **pear** (b) **date** (c) **apple**

______ 6. Genus *Ananas*, a bromeliad, succulent and fleshy fruit

(a) **papaya** (b) **orange** (c) **pineapple**

______ 7. Genus *Musa*, an elongated tropical fruit, fleshy pulp, yellow or red rind

(a) **banana** (b) **mango** (c) **tamarind**

______ 8. Oblong fruit of a palm, genus *Phoenix*

(a) **fig** (b) **date** (c) **palmetto**

______ 9. *Citrus aurantfolia*, a greenish-yellow fruit with acidic juicy pulp

(a) **lime** (b) **lemon** (c) **kumquat**

______ 10. Thick-skinned red fruit full of many tart seeds, genus *Punica*

(a) **papaya** (b) **plum** (c) **pomegranate**

Fruit Bowl Recipe Choose four of the fruits listed on this page. Invent a recipe using these four fruits. Write the recipe on the back of this sheet of paper.

Name ______________________________ Date ______________

Vegetable Truths

Read each statement. Circle **T** if it is true, **F** if it is false. For each statement that you mark **F**, turn the sheet of paper over and write a correct definition of the boldfaced word. You may use a dictionary.

T F 1. The word **vegetable** refers to any plant.

T F 2. A **crookneck** is a type of nut.

T F 3. A **nut** is a hard-shelled dry fruit or seed.

T F 4. A **rutabaga** is slender like a parsnip.

T F 5. A **muskmelon** is a watermelon.

T F 6. The word **vegetable** refers to a plant that humans eat, usually as part of a meal.

T F 7. **Peanuts** are legumes.

T F 8. **Peas** are legumes.

T F 9. The word **cantaloupe** comes from *Cantalupo*, a former papal villa near Rome.

T F 10. **Carob** is a root that grows underground.

T F 11. **Almonds** grow on vines.

T F 12. **Collards** are kale plants.

T F 13. A **parsley** plant is a young parsnip plant.

T F 14. **Sweet potatoes** belong to the morning glory family of vines.

T F 15. The tubers of the **Jerusalem artichoke** are used as food.

Vegetable List Number a separate sheet of paper from 1 to 50. Next to each number, write the name of a different vegetable. How close to fifty can you come?

Name ______________________________ Date ______________

Vegetable Classification

You will need a dictionary (and perhaps an encyclopedia) in order to complete the activity below. Write each of the twenty-five vegetables (one of them is listed twice) under the proper category, depending on which part of the vegetable we eat. (For example, ***pumpkin*** would go under the Fruit category, since a pumpkin is the fruit of the pumpkin vine.)

artichoke	**carrot**	**kale**	**rhubarb**
asparagus	**cauliflower**	**leek**	**spinach**
beans	**celery**	**lettuce**	**tomato**
beet	**collards**	**okra**	**turnip**
broccoli	**cucumber**	**parsnip**	**watermelon**
cabbage	**eggplant**	**radish**	**zucchini**

	ROOTS	LEAVES	FRUITS
1.	________	________	________
2.	________	________	________
3.	________	________	________
4.	________	________	________
5.	________	________	________

	STALKS OR STEMS	FLOWERS OR PODS
1.	________	________
2.	________	________
3.	________	________
4.	________	________
5.	________	________

Tomato Trouble In 1893, the United States Supreme Court handed down a decision on the tomato! The case was based on the following circumstances. The United States had imposed a tariff on all imported vegetables, but not on imported fruits. Tomato growers from another country said that since the tomato is the fruit of the tomato plant, a tomato is a fruit, not a vegetable, and therefore tomatoes should not be subject to the tariff. Think about this. What is a fruit? What is a vegetable? Imagine that you were sitting on the Supreme Court. Write a one-page summary of what your decision would be.

Name ______________________________ Date ______________

Spices, Herbs, and Flavorings

Write the letter of the correct answer next to each brief definition. You may use a dictionary.

______	1. spice named because it seems to combine the taste of several spices	a. **cinnamon**
______	2. herb from the mint family; leaves are used to flavor tomatoes and many Italian foods	b. **sage**
______	3. yellowish-brown spice from the inner bark of the cassia tree; used in pastries	c. **horseradish**
______	4. herb whose seeds and leaves are used to flavor foods, particularly pickles	d. **allspice**
______	5. tall herb of parsley family whose licorice-flavored seeds are used as seasoning	e. **parsley**
______	6. aromatic plant whose roots are crushed for spice; used in pastries and soda pop	f. **dill**
______	7. plant of mustard family; pungent roots are so strong they can make your eyes water	g. **ginger**
______	8. hot, sharp-tasting yellow spice made from ground seeds of this plant	h. **mustard**
______	9. hard seed grated and used as a spice	i. **oregano**
______	10. plant of mint family whose leaves are used as a spice, especially in pizza	j. **basil**
______	11. herb whose leaves are eaten raw or used in soups and other dishes; a breath sweetener	k. **fennel**
______	12. aromatic leaves used in meats and stuffing	l. **nutmeg**

Expensive Spice At the library, read about saffron. On a separate sheet of paper, write three paragraphs about saffron. Explain where it comes from, how it is used, and why it is such an expensive spice.

Name ________________________________ Date ________________

Step Right Up

Read the speech below. Then, on a separate sheet of paper, write each of the boldfaced words. Next to each word, write its definition. Wherever possible, include the name of the plant the product comes from and what it is used for. You may use a dictionary.

Step right up, folks!

Step right up and hear about the wonderful world of plants!

Why, if it weren't for plants, we wouldn't be alive!

Think of the clothes you wear. Think of **cotton**, **flax**, and **kapok**.

Think of how plant materials aid us. Think of **hemp**, **jute**, and **sisal**.

And that's not all, no sirree!

Of course there's paper, but there's also **cork**, **rubber**, **resin**, and **latex**.

Don't forget **turpentine** and **charcoal**.

And what about food, hmmm?

What about grains and vegetables and fruits and spices and herbs?

What about sugar and coffee and tea and chocolate and maple syrup?

Feeling ill?

What about **witch hazel** and **camphor**?

What about **penicillin**, for that matter—it comes from a mold.

And where would doctors be without **digitalis**?

Yes, sir, ma'am, and ms.—where would we be without plants?

Plant Speech Choose one of the boldfaced words on this page. Look up information on the product in the library. Then give a three- to five-minute speech explaining how this product is obtained from plants and what its uses are.

Name ______________________________ Date ______________

Twenty Flowers

Begonia, carnation, chrysanthemum, crocus, daffodil, dahlia, daisy, iris, lavender, lilac, lily, lotus, marigold, peony, petunia, phlox, rose, sunflower, tulip, zinnia – these words are hidden below. The words run from left to right or from top to bottom. Circle each of the twenty words.

D	H	L	O	R	V	Y	E	X	M	A	R	I	G	O	L	D	U
E	N	K	G	D	C	B	B	F	J	M	O	Q	T	W	Z	A	T
A	E	I	A	A	P	P	E	O	N	Y	S	S	I	A	Z	H	W
Z	I	N	N	I	A	T	G	Q	M	J	E	F	B	C	G	L	K
N	E	U	X	S	E	Y	O	V	R	O	L	S	H	D	A	I	B
C	C	H	R	Y	S	A	N	T	H	E	M	U	M	D	E	A	F
G	H	I	J	K	L	A	I	M	N	O	R	N	E	P	D	Q	S
T	U	V	C	A	R	N	A	T	I	O	N	F	I	W	A	X	L
Y	L	C	A	Z	E	D	C	B	A	H	G	L	F	E	F	I	O
J	I	R	I	S	K	L	P	H	L	O	X	O	O	N	F	M	T
A	L	O	P	Q	L	E	R	S	T	A	V	W	I	W	O	Y	U
E	A	C	Z	Q	I	S	P	Q	T	E	U	E	R	V	D	O	S
N	C	U	M	A	L	A	V	E	N	D	E	R	I	J	I	K	L
E	A	S	B	F	Y	C	G	D	H	L	O	K	T	U	L	I	P
N	M	Q	P	E	T	U	N	I	A	A	P	S	P	T	U	E	R

Flower Power In literature, flowers have often been used as symbols. On the back of this sheet of paper, define the word *symbol*. Then write a paragraph telling what you think the **rose** and the **lily** might be used as symbols of in literature.

Name ______________________________ Date ____________________

Animal Homes

Fill in the blanks below by writing the correct word on each line. You may use the dictionary.

den	lair	aerie	lodge	cocoon
cave	nest	hive	burrow	warren

1. The resting or living place of a wild animal such as a cougar, lion, or tiger is a(n) ______________________.
2. A container that houses bees is a(n) ______________________.
3. A nest on a cliff or mountain top, particularly an eagle's nest, is a(n) ______________________.
4. A(n) ______________________ is an excavation in the ground made by an animal such as a woodchuck or prairie dog for shelter.
5. An already-existing natural rock chamber or underground chamber, a(n) ______________________ can be used as an animal home.
6. The term ______________________ is a general term for an animal home—it includes caves, hollows, caverns, and lairs.
7. The area or structure where rabbits live is a(n) ______________________.
8. A(n) ______________________ is the home of a beaver or muskrat.
9. A bed or container made by a bird to house its eggs and young is a(n) ______________________.
10. A(n) ______________________ is the home of an insect larva while it passes through the pupa stage.

Lodge Drawing Use the library to find information on what an animal lodge looks like and how it is constructed. On a separate sheet of paper draw a diagram showing a cross-section of a lodge. Label the parts of the diagram.

Name ______________________________ Date ______________

Fish Puzzle

Solve the crossword puzzle by writing the correct word in each blank. You may use a dictionary.

Down

1. the fin on a fish's back
3. the small flat plates that cover a fish
4. Fish use these to move and swim.
6. the largest of all fish
7. adjective used to name salt-water fish
8. When a fish produces eggs or young, it ______ .

Across

2. common fish found everywhere; no scales, a scavenger
5. the eggs of a fish
9. Fish breathe through these.
10. Fish were the first ______ , or animals with backbones.
11. flatfish that lives on the bottom of the ocean bed; has both eyes on topside of head
12. Fish that eat debris and dead things are called ______ .

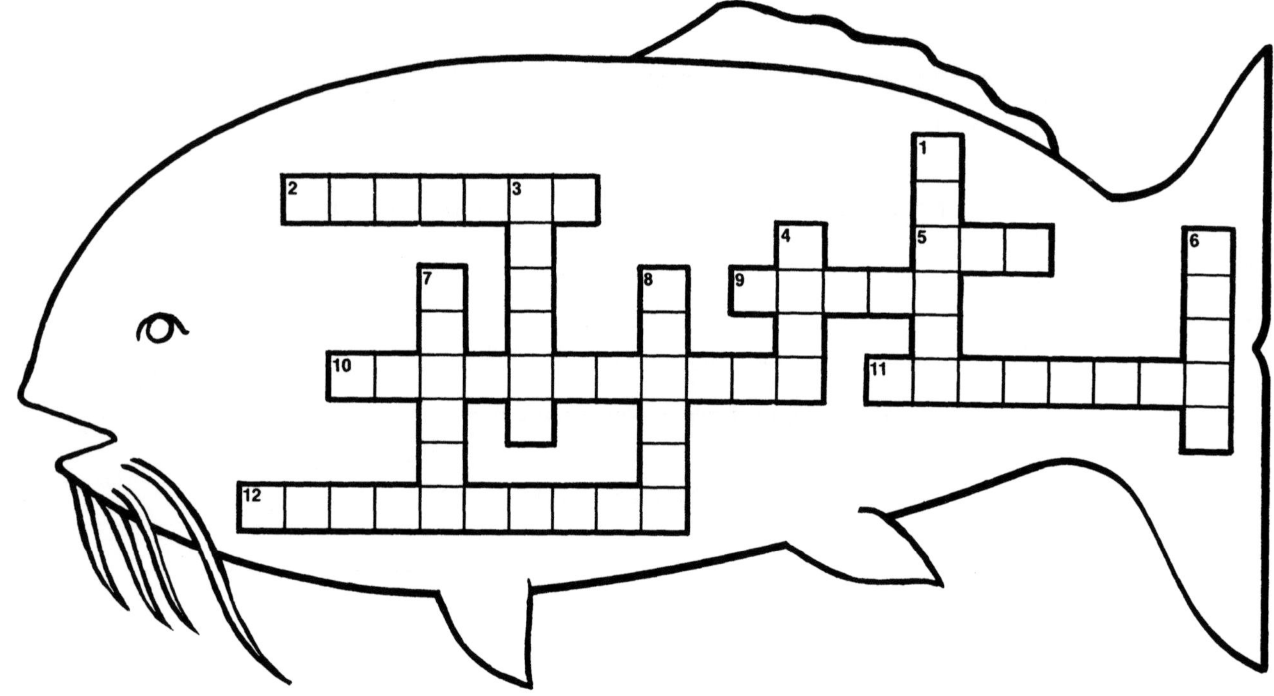

Fish Graph Choose three different kinds of fish (for example, tuna, salmon, and herring) and research how many tons of them are caught each year. Make a bar graph that shows the annual tonnage caught of each of the three fish both this year and the previous year.

Name ______________________________ Date ______________

Animal Young

f o a l k i t t e n l e v e r e t p u p j o e y g o s l i n g

There are twelve words in the letters at the top and bottom of this page. Separate the letters into words; then write the correct word on each line below. You may use a dictionary.

1. A young goose is a ______________________ .
2. A young goat is a ______________________ .
3. A young beaver or cat is a ______________________ .
4. A young deer, moose, or elk is a ______________________ .
5. A young elephant or cow is a ______________________ .
6. A young bear or wolf is a ______________________ .
7. A young seal is a ______________________ .
8. A young hare is a ______________________ .
9. A young sheep is a ______________________ .
10. A young camel or horse is a ______________________ .
11. A young kangaroo is a ______________________ .
12. A young fish is a ______________________ .

c u b l a m b k i d f i n g e r l i n g f a w n c a l f

Whale of a Baby At the library, read about whales. Write two paragraphs giving information about the size of a newborn whale, the amount of food it eats, its growth, and how the mother cares for it.

Name ______________________________ Date ______________________

Horse Facts

Study the diagram below. Write the correct vocabulary word on each line of the diagram. You may use the dictionary.

hock	hoof	croup	cannon	muzzle	shoulder
dock	mane	flank	fetlock	forelock	withers

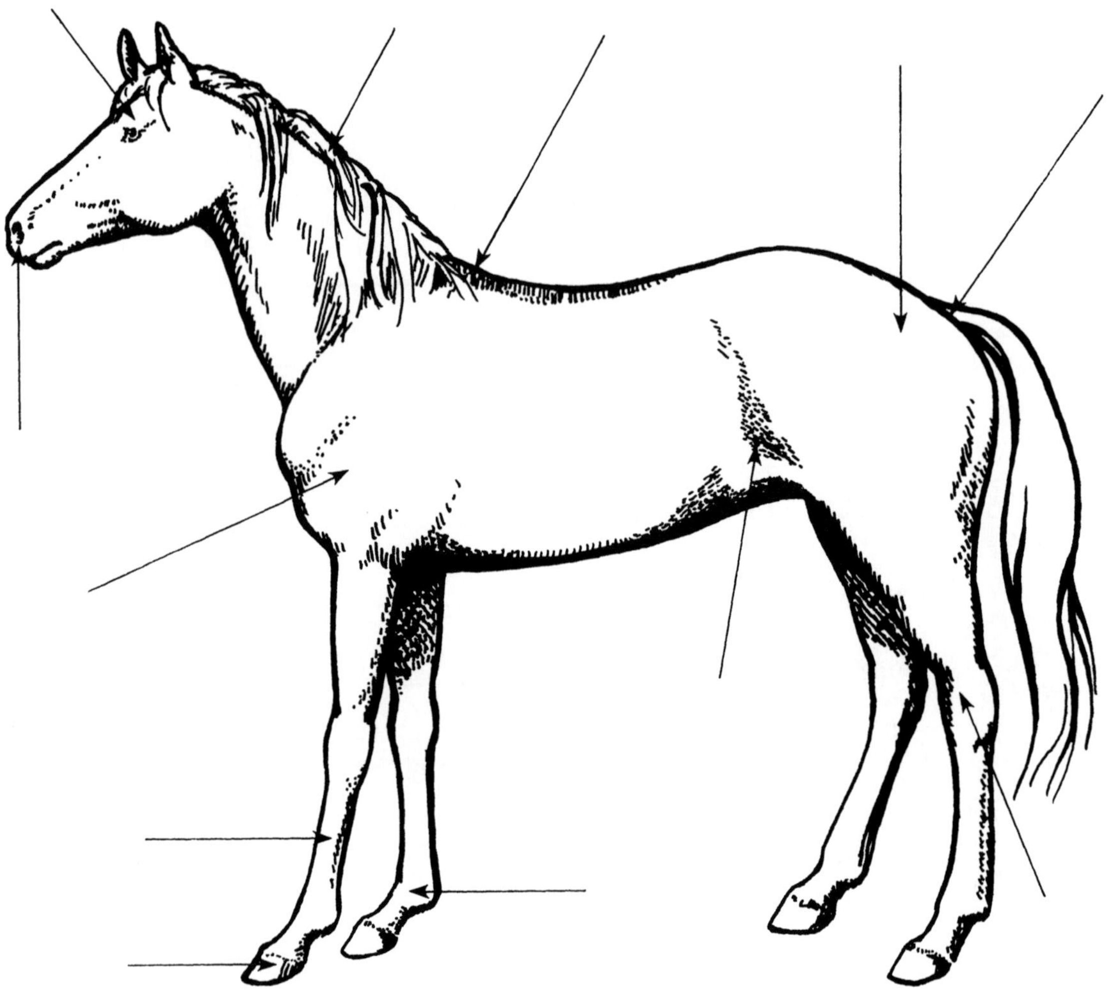

Horse Idioms The English language has several "horse" idioms. On a separate sheet of paper, explain what each of these five idiomatic expressions means. You may use a dictionary. **(1) That's a horse of another color. (2) Don't put the cart before the horse. (3) Get off your high horse. (4) Hold your horses. (5) I got it straight from the horse's mouth.**

Name ________________________ Date ____________

Reptile Word Parts

Each vocabulary word below has been broken into two parts. The first part is in Column 1 and the second part is in Column 2. Put the word parts together correctly. Write the correct word next to each brief definition or description. You may use a dictionary.

		1	2
________	1. large, thick-skinned, long-bodied reptile, lives in tropical waters	**di**	**odile**
		tur	**leon**
________	2. large constrictor snake		
________	3. group of extinct reptiles	**geck**	**tiles**
________	4. largest poisonous snake	**liz**	**thon**
________	5. small tropical lizard, eats insects	**rep**	**tles**
________	6. the class of air-breathing vertebrates that includes snakes	**igua**	**nosaurs**
________	7. tropical American lizard, eats plants, used as food by natives	**chame**	**o**
________	8. order of reptiles covered with hard protective plate	**crock**	**bra**
________	9. lizard whose skin can change color	**co**	**ards**
________	10. group of reptiles, fastest moving of all reptiles, not large in size, four limbs	**py**	**na**

Dinosaur Definitions On the other side of this sheet of paper, define each of these terms: ***ichthyosaur***, ***plesiosaur***, ***pterosaur***, ***thecodont***, ***sauropod***, ***theropod***, ***stegosaur***.

Name ______________________ Date ______________

Which Group?

Ant, auk, bat, butterfly, chameleon, eel, frog, goby, mussel, octopus, owl, puffin, salamander, scorpion, shark, snail, snake, spider, squirrel, tick, toad, turtle, wasp, whale – each of these animals belongs to one of the groups listed. First, write a definition of each group word. Then put each animal into its correct group. You may use a dictionary.

1. **MAMMALS** are ______________________

   ____

   Examples: ________ ________ ________

2. **REPTILES** are ______________________

   ____

   Examples: ________ ________ ________

3. **AMPHIBIANS** are ______________________

   ____

   Examples: ________ ________ ________

4. **FISH** are ______________________

   ____

   Examples: ________ ________ ________

5. **BIRDS** are ______________________

   ____

   Examples: ________ ________ ________

6. **INSECTS** are ______________________

   ____

   Examples: ________ ________ ________

7. **ARACHNIDS** are ______________________

   ____

   Examples: ________ ________ ________

8. **MOLLUSKS** are ______________________

   ____

   Examples: ________ ________ ________

Animal Fable Choose one of the animals listed on this page and write a fable about it.

Name ______________________________ Date ______________

Omnivorous Words

Write the letter of the correct answer next to each brief definition. You may use a dictionary.

______	1. animal that lives on garbage, carrion	a. **cud**
______	2. cone-shaped, pointed teeth	b. **herbivorous**
______	3. food brought up into the mouth from first stomach and chewed again	c. **browse**
______	4. to feed on herbage such as grass	d. **gnaw**
______	5. feeding on both animals and vegetables	e. **scavenger**
______	6. to rechew food that was swallowed and has been brought up again	f. **carnivorous**
______	7. feeding only on animal matter	g. **ruminate**
______	8. to dig in the earth with the snout	h. **root**
______	9. to feed on tender leaves, twigs, and shoots of trees and shrubs	i. **canines**
______	10. dead and putrifying flesh fed on by animals such as buzzards	j. **omnivorous**
______	11. to chew on with the teeth	k. **carrion**
______	12. feeding only on vegetable matter	l. **graze**

Double Duty Some of the words in the above word list (***browse***, for example) have more than one meaning. List these words on the back of this page and write their other definition(s) beside them.

Name ______________________________ Date ______________

Listen!

Animals make many sounds. They grunt, growl, coo, hiss, bellow, neigh, whinny, nicker, bugle, low, and chirp. They howl, bark, croak, peep, whine, bleat, blat, hoot, cluck, squeak, twitter, scream, and yap. They chirr, crow, boom, rattle, bray, and whistle. They honk, squawk, roar, caw, chirp, scold, chatter, bawl, trumpet, gobble, squeal, and wail.

Unscramble each verb below to tell what sound each animal makes. You may use a dictionary.

1. owl	**toho**	_ _ _ _
2. duck	**cakuq**	_ _ _ _ _
3. cow	**owl**	_ _ _
4. rooster	**worc**	_ _ _ _
5. elephant	**prettum**	_ _ _ _ _ _ _
6. frog	**korac**	_ _ _ _ _
7. sheep	**table**	_ _ _ _ _
8. horse	**inwhyn**	_ _ _ _ _ _
9. donkey	**yarb**	_ _ _ _
10. pigeon	**oco**	_ _ _
11. goose	**nokh**	_ _ _ _
12. fox	**pay**	_ _ _
13. cricket	**phirc**	_ _ _ _ _
14. squirrel	**thratec**	_ _ _ _ _ _ _
15. eagle	**macers**	_ _ _ _ _ _
16. chipmunk	**richr**	_ _ _ _ _
17. wolf	**wohl**	_ _ _ _
18. pig	**untrg**	_ _ _ _ _
19. bear	**wrogl**	_ _ _ _ _
20. snake	**shis**	_ _ _ _

Night Out Imagine that you are spending a night in a tent in the wilderness. Write two paragraphs describing the sounds you hear.

Name ______________________________ Date ______________

Bird Sounds

Each bird word below is spelled the way it sounds. (Dictionaries give these phonetic spellings after each word.) After each phonetic spelling, write the actual spelling of the word. Write the letter of the correct definition in front of each number. You may use a dictionary.

______ 1. **mäk in bərd** _ _ _ _ _ _ _ _ _ _ _ _ _

______ 2. **jăk dô** _ _ _ _ _ _ _ _ _

______ 3. **kē wē** _ _ _ _

______ 4. **ren** _ _ _ _

______ 5. **ôk** _ _ _

______ 6. **kookə burə** _ _ _ _ _ _ _ _ _ _ _ _ _

______ 7. **krān** _ _ _ _ _

______ 8. **to͞o kan** _ _ _ _ _ _ _

______ 9. **sand pī pər** _ _ _ _ _ _ _ _ _ _ _ _

______ 10. **kwāl** _ _ _ _ _

a. an Australian kingfisher
b. brightly colored large-beaked fruit-eating bird of tropical America
c. migratory game bird of Old and New World; bobwhite
d. bird of southern United States that imitates notes of other birds
e. small songbird that eats insects, has a long bill and rounded wings
f. small shorebird related to snipe but with larger bill
g. tailless New Zealand bird with undeveloped wings and long bill
h. large wading bird with very long legs and neck and long, straight bill
i. diving bird of northern seas with heavy body, webbed feet
j. European blackbird related to crow but smaller; grackle

Bird List Number a separate sheet of paper from 1 to 50. List as many different birds as you can. How close to fifty can you come?

Name ______________________ Date ______________

Cover-up

Animals have different coverings. Circle the one word in each row that tells what the covering of that animal (or animals) is called. You may use a dictionary.

1. beaver, fox	**scales**	**fur**	**forage**
2. sheep	**whorls**	**chitin**	**wool**
3. porcupine	**cartilage**	**forage**	**spines**
4. human	**skin**	**vibrissae**	**ruff**
5. mussel	**mane**	**shell**	**cartilage**
6. bird	**vibrissae**	**mane**	**feathers**
7. fish	**scales**	**armor**	**hide**
8. armadillo	**ruff**	**spines**	**armor**
9. insect	**chitin**	**vibrissae**	**shell**
10. elephant	**cartilage**	**armor**	**hide**

Choose Your Covering If you could choose your outside covering, which kind would you choose? Write one paragraph giving the reasons for your choice.

Name ______________________ Date ______________

Animal Analysis

Write an answer to each question below. You may use the dictionary.

1. What do an **addax** and an **oryx** have in common? ______________________

2. What is an **okapi**? ______________________

3. What do a **serval**, **lynx**, and **ocelot** have in common? ______________________

4. How does a **dromedary** differ from a **Bactrian camel**? ______________________

5. Are **chuckwallas** and **newts** related? ______________________

6. What do a **manatee**, **dormouse**, and **tapir** have in common? ______________________

7. Explain why a **bongo** would not run into a **guanaco** naturally. ______________________

8. What do a **wombat**, **platypus**, and **emu** have in common? ______________________

Animal Questions Write two questions of your own similar to those above. Use at least two animals in each question. Make certain that the question can be answered by consulting a dictionary. Write the answer to each question. Choose animals from this list: **alpaca, echidna, ferret, gibbon, ibex, jerboa, lemur, llama, osprey, rhea, wahoo, whelk, zebu.**

Name ________________________________ Date ____________________

False Colors

Read each sentence below and think about the definition of the boldfaced word. Circle **T** if a statement is true. Circle **F** if it is false. If the sentence is false, write a correct definition of the boldfaced word on the back of this sheet of paper. You may use a dictionary.

T **F** 1. A **roan** is an animal such as a horse whose coat could be red, black, or brown, thickly sprinkled with white or gray.

T **F** 2. **Dun** is a color similar to deep, rich crimson.

T **F** 3. An animal that is **grizzly** has a coat flecked with gray, silver, or white.

T **F** 4. A **pinto** is a horse with irregular markings of color.

T **F** 5. **Piebald** refers to an animal such as the arctic fox whose color changes each winter and summer.

T **F** 6. A **dappled** animal is one whose coat is spotted with a second color.

T **F** 7. **Brindled** refers to an animal with white patches around its eyes.

T **F** 8. **Tawny** refers to an animal such as a cat which is light brown to brownish orange in color.

T **F** 9. A **calico** animal is one whose coat has large blotches of color.

T **F** 10. Animals whose coloring helps them blend into their surroundings are concealed by **camouflage**.

Pied Poem Read "Pied Beauty," a short poem by Gerard Manley Hopkins. On a separate sheet of paper, write a one-paragraph summary of what Hopkins says in the poem.

Name ______________________________ Date ______________

Insect Compounds

Each insect word on this page is a compound word—one word made out of two separate words (such as *fire* + *fly* = *firefly*). Make the names of eight insects by combining one word from the left wing with one word from the right wing. Write each word on a line; then write a definition telling what kind of insect each word names. You may use a dictionary.

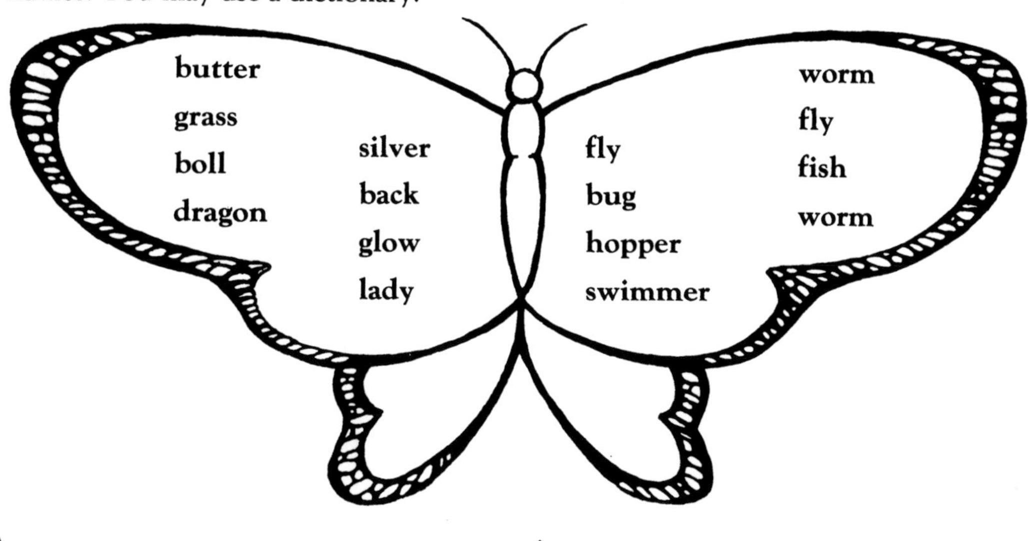

1. A______________________ is ______________________
____
2. A______________________ is ______________________
____
3. A______________________ is ______________________
____
4. A______________________ is ______________________
____
5. A______________________ is ______________________
____
6. A______________________ is ______________________
____
7. A______________________ is ______________________
____
8. A______________________ is ______________________
____

Silk Subject At the library, read an encyclopedia article about the silkworm. On a separate sheet of paper, write three paragraphs on the silkworm and the silk industry.

Name ______________________________ Date ______________

Animal Weapons

Antlers, claws, fangs, hoofs, horns, nails, quills, talons, teeth, tusks, venom – these are some of the weapons animals use to attack other animals and/or to defend themselves. Write each word in the correct space in the puzzle. You may use a dictionary.

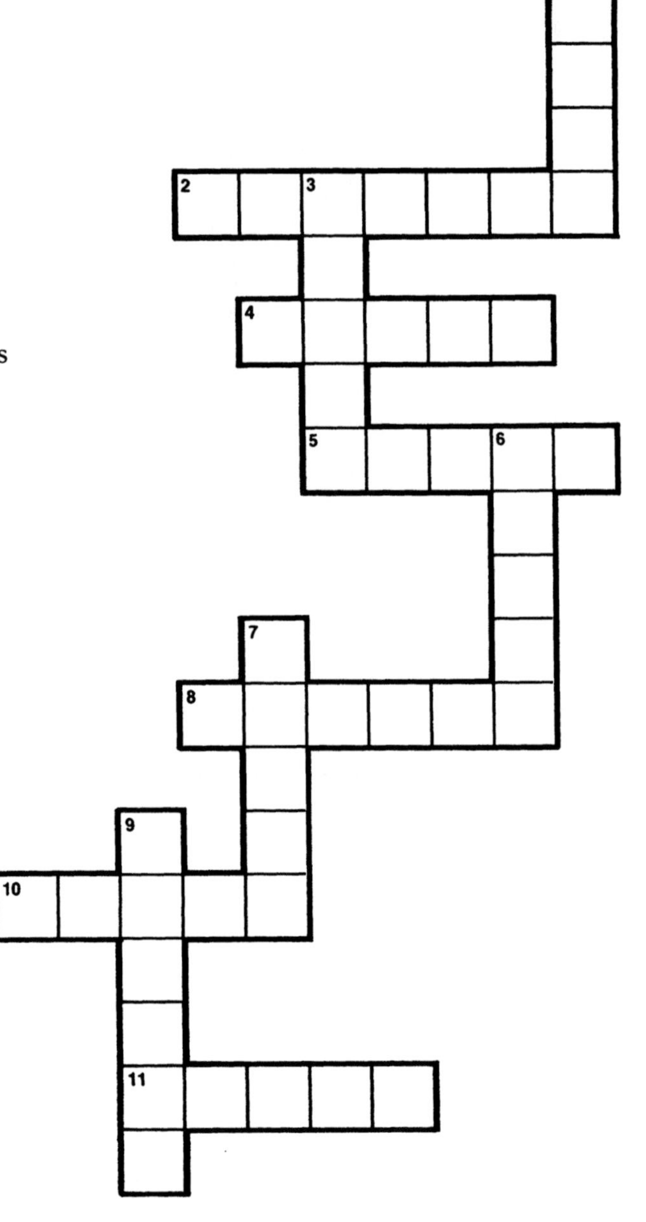

Across

2. used by deer, moose, wapiti
4. used by some snakes, scorpions, and spiders
5. used by a horse
8. used by a porcupine
10. used by bears and cats
11. used by ostriches, rabbits, kangaroos

Down

1. used by goats, sheep, water buffalo
3. used by dogs, wolves, mice, rats
6. used by snakes, tigers
7. used by walrus, elephant, warthog
9. used by owls, hawks, eagles

Animal Speech Use the library to research the subject of abuse to animals. Prepare a three-minute speech on the subject of animal abuse. Tell what it is, give examples of it, and discuss what can be done to prevent it.

Name ____ Date ____________________

Creature Characteristics

Each of the boldfaced words below is an adjective that refers to an animal-like characteristic. Read each statement, then circle the word that is the answer. You may use a dictionary.

1. If you wanted to tell your friend that he swam like a fish, would you call his swimming **piscine** or **ophidian**?

2. Would you call a graceful person **porcine** or **feline**?

3. If you wanted to compliment your friend on her courage, would you call her actions **vulpine** or **leonine**?

4. If you were writing a science fiction story featuring a race of limbless creatures as the heros, would these creatures be **bovine** or **ophidian**?

5. Would a large, shambling, hairy person be called **ursine** or **ovine**?

6. If you were testifying against a cunning thief in court, would you describe the thief as **pachydermous** or **vulpine**?

7. Would a heavy, greedy character in a novel best be described as **porcine** or **piscine**?

8. Your young brother and sister trustingly follow you wherever you go and do whatever you ask—are they **ovine** or **ursine**?

9. **Leonine** or **pachydermous**—which is the correct word to describe a person with the characteristics of a rhinoceros?

10. **Lupine** or **bovine**—which is the correct word to describe a person who eats ravenously?

Animal Farm Read George Orwell's *Animal Farm*. Write a report on the characteristics that Orwell gives each kind of animal.

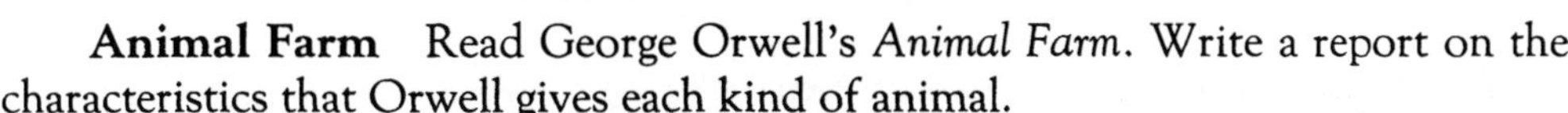

Name ______________________________ Date ______________

Vital Organs

All the words below name parts (specific or general) of the human body. Look up each word in a dictionary. Write a definition for each word. Then write terms 3–10 in the appropriate spaces in the diagram.

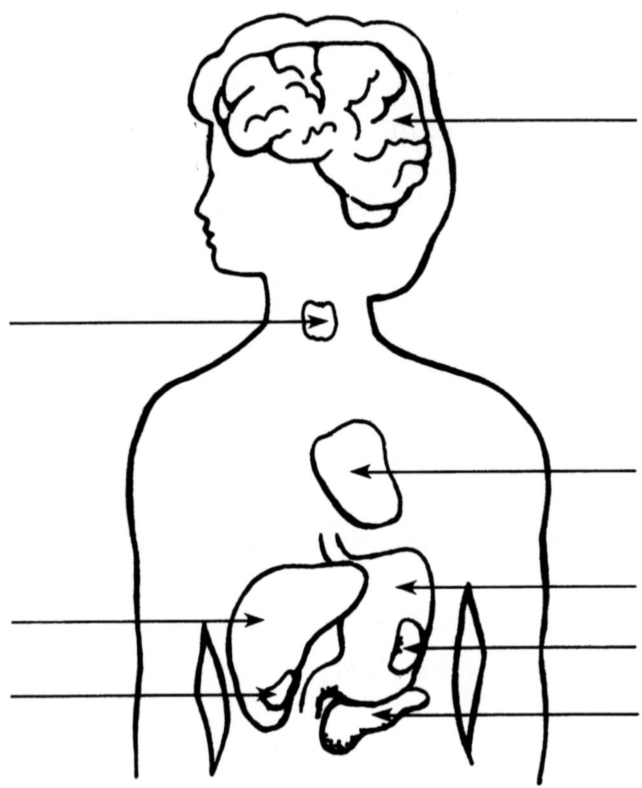

1. **organ** ______________________________
2. **gland** ______________________________
3. **heart** ______________________________
4. **spleen** ______________________________
5. **brain** ______________________________
6. **gallbladder** ______________________________
7. **pancreas** ______________________________
8. **liver** ______________________________
9. **stomach** ______________________________
10. **thyroid** ______________________________

Pancreas Parts At least twenty-five different words can be made out of the letters in the word ***pancreas***. Write ***pancreas*** on the back of this sheet of paper. Then write all the words you can make out of the letters present in ***pancreas***.

Name ______________________________ Date ______________

Hands Down

Study the two drawings below. Write the correct vocabulary word on each line of the drawings. You may use a dictionary.

knuckle	**cuticle**	**web**	**finger pad**
lifeline	**palm**	**heel**	**index finger**
fingertip	**fingernail**	**digit**	**wrist**

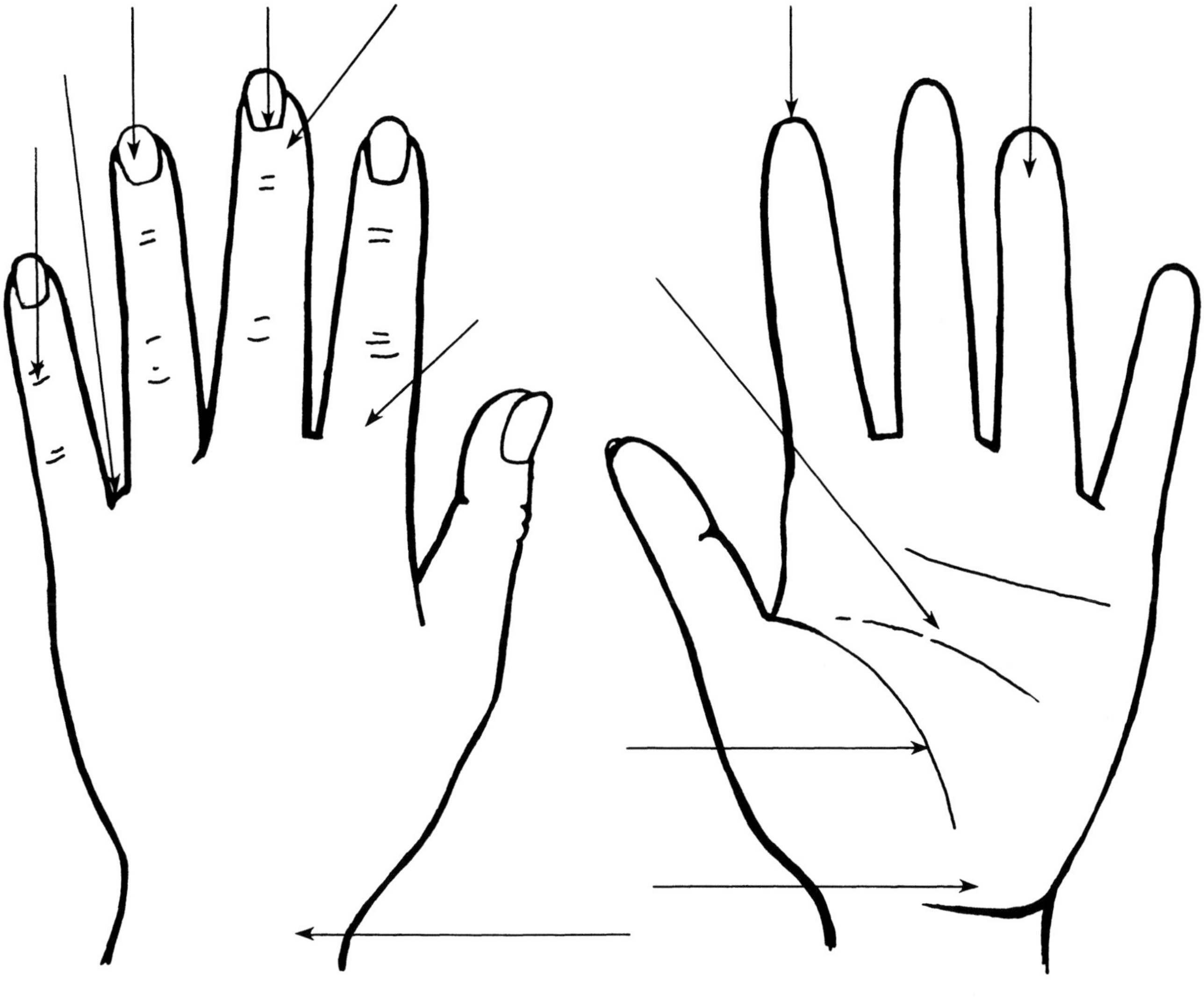

Hand Idioms Many expressions in the English language contain the word ***hand***. On a separate sheet of paper, explain what each of the following idioms or sayings means: (1) **hand over fist**; (2) **hands down**; (3) **hand in glove**; (4) **A bird in the hand is worth two in the bush**; (5) **Many hands make light work.**

Name ________________________________ Date ____________________

A Real Dig

Many bones in the human body have both a common name and a scientific name. Read the story below. Next to each boldfaced common name for a bone, write its scientific name. The scientific names are: **carpals, clavicle, coccyx, femurs, humerus, mandible, patella, pelvis, scapula, sternum, tarsals, tibia.**

What a find! Up until this time, the two young archaeologists had found only shards of pottery. But now in front of them lay a grimy but perfect human skeleton!

"Look at the **jawbone** ____________________!" exclaimed Derek. "It's absolutely perfect! And so is the **upper-arm bone** ____________________."

"That's not all!" shouted Gwendolyn. "The **wrist bones** ____________________ aren't even broken! And the **breastbone** ____________________ is intact!" Carefully, she flicked some dust off the **collarbone** ____________________. "Will you look at the **shoulder blade** ____________________ and the **hip bone** ____________________!" she said enthusiastically. "I haven't seen such a good specimen since college biology." Through the hip bones, Gwen could see the **tail bone** ____________________, also intact.

"Hmm," said Derek. "He must have been a tall man. Look at the length of the **thighbones** ____________________. He wasn't an athlete—no broken **kneecap** ____________________. Look, Gwen! All the **ankle bones** ____________________ are still there! Wait. . .there's something on the **shin-bone** ____________________. It's *writing*," groaned Derek. "And it says, 'PROPERTY OF UNIVERSITY BIOLOGY DEPARTMENT.' We've been tricked, Gwen!"

Revenge of the Archaeologists On a separate sheet of paper, write a story telling how Gwendolyn and Derek respond to this trick.

Name ______________________________ Date ______________

What's the System?

Read each definition below. Write the letter of the correct body system on each line. You may use a dictionary.

_____ 1. This system provides a framework of support for the rest of your body and helps give you shape.
(a) **endocrine** (b) **skeletal** (c) **sensory**

_____ 2. This system helps you move.
(a) **circulatory** (b) **digestive** (c) **muscular**

_____ 3. This system turns your food into fuel.
(a) **reproductive** (b) **nervous** (c) **digestive**

_____ 4. This system supplies oxygen to the body.
(a) **respiratory** (b) **endocrine** (c) **urinary**

_____ 5. This system carries fuel and oxygen to all parts of the body.
(a) **circulatory** (b) **muscular** (c) **sensory**

_____ 6. This system helps remove wastes from the body.
(a) **digestive** (b) **circulatory** (c) **urinary**

_____ 7. This system reports to your brain what is happening in and around you.
(a) **endocrine** (b) **sensory** (c) **reproductive**

_____ 8. The brain sends instructions to your muscles, glands, and organs through this system.
(a) **reproductive** (b) **sensory** (c) **nervous**

_____ 9. This system sends hormones through your bloodstream.
(a) **endocrine** (b) **respiratory** (c) **circulatory**

_____ 10. This system helps create a new human being.
(a) **nervous** (b) **reproductive** (c) **sensory**

Definitions Make Sense On the back of this sheet of paper, write and define each of the following words: **sensational, sense, sensibility, sensible, sensitive, sensitize, sensor.**

Name ______________________________ Date ______________

Hidden Bites

Bicuspid, canine, cavity, crown, cuspid, dentin, enamel, gum, incisor, molar, plaque, pulp – these words are hidden below, one in each row. Read each clue, then circle the one word in each row that goes with the clue. You may use a dictionary.

Clue	Letters
1. firm tissue around base of teeth	I N C I G R E A G U M C A V C R O W E X
2. a tooth adapted for cutting	E N C A G U B I L D E N T I N C I S O R
3. pitted area in a tooth, caused by decay	C U C A V I T Y T E E C G U D E N M O L
4. soft, inner part of tooth	P U L P I L L O E R B I C U D E N T M O
5. hard substance covering exposed part of tooth	C R O C A N I B I C U S I E N A M E L R
6. tooth having one point, same as a canine	G U R U E C R U C U S P I D E X B R O K
7. the part of a tooth outside the gum line	R O O N E C R O W N B I C A R I Y G U I
8. conical tooth between incisors and bicuspids	E N A M P L A G U I N C A N I N E R E T
9. a tooth having two points	A B I C U S P I D P L C A V I N C I S G
10. thin film of mucus on a tooth surface	P R E C L U P L A Q U E I N G Q U I R Z
11. part of tooth containing pulp and root canals	C R O D E N T I N E N A P U L C U S P I
12. tooth with a broad crown for grinding food	C A V T O O H E M E N M O L A R M O U T

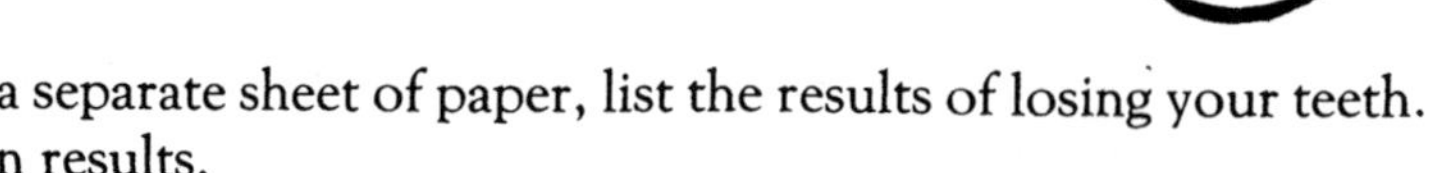

Tooth List On a separate sheet of paper, list the results of losing your teeth. Try to list at least seven results.

Name ________________________________ Date ______________

Rhymes With

Read each definition below. Write the answer on the line. The answer rhymes with the boldfaced word. (Remember that words that rhyme are not always spelled similarly.) You may use the dictionary.

1. A sudden, acute failure of the body's circulatory functions.

   Rhymes with **clock**. _ _ _ _ _

2. A habitual muscular contraction (of the eye, for example).

   Rhymes with **pick**. _ _ _

3. A scraped or worn area (of the skin, for example).

   Rhymes with **occasion**. _ _ _ _ _ _ _ _

4. Free from bacteria or other microorganisms.

   Rhymes with **peril**. _ _ _ _ _ _ _

5. Not malignant.

   Rhymes with **confine**. _ _ _ _ _ _

6. A sac containing fluid or semisolid matter.

   Rhymes with **mist**. _ _ _ _

7. An injury in which the skin is not broken.

   Rhymes with **cruise**. _ _ _ _ _ _

8. The protrusion of an organ through the wall that normally contains it.

   Rhymes with **Calpurnia**. _ _ _ _ _ _

9. A drug that kills the growth of bacteria.

   Rhymes with **psychotic**. _ _ _ _ _ _ _ _ _ _

10. Surgical removal of small bits of tissue for study under a microscope.

    Rhymes with **dropsy**. _ _ _ _ _ _

Rhyme Time Write a rhyming poem of three stanzas using at least three of the words from this list.

Name ______________________________ Date ______________

Muscle Words

Study the two drawings below. Write the correct vocabulary word or term on each line of the drawings. You may use a dictionary. The muscle words are: **biceps, deltoid, gastrocnemius, hamstring, latissimus dorsi, pectoralis major, quadriceps, sartorius, trapezius, triceps.**

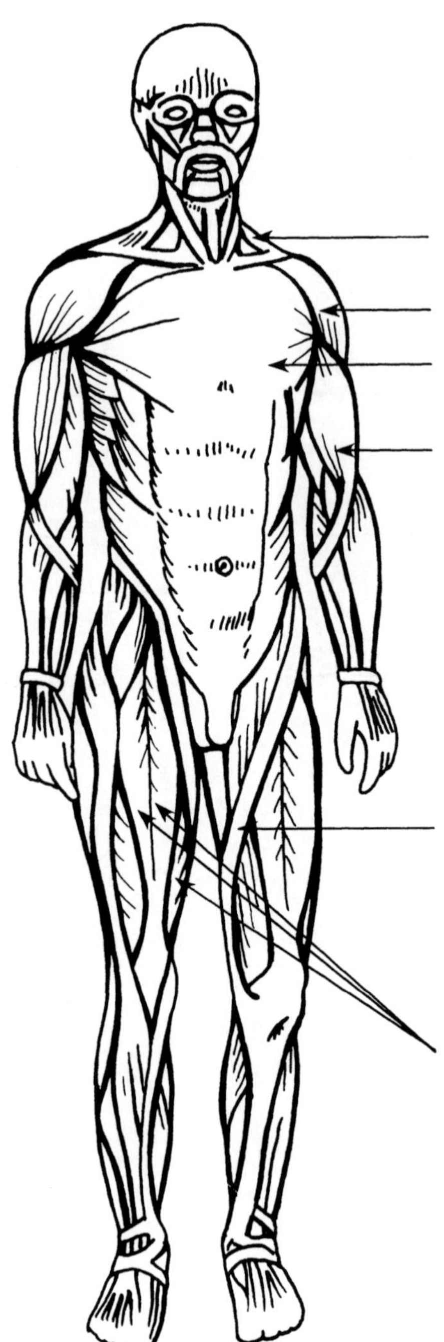

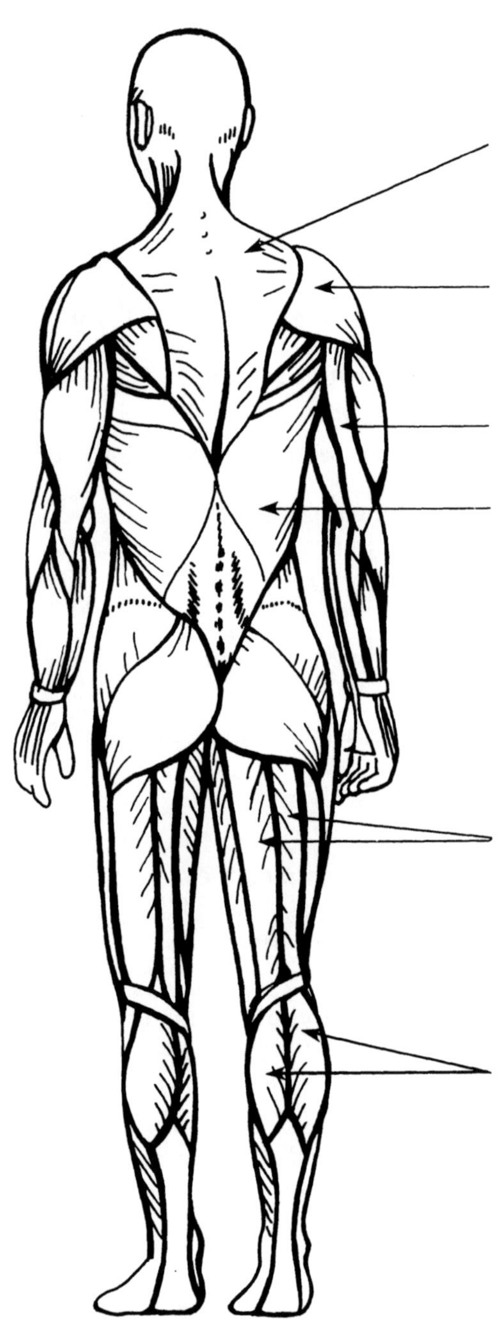

Muscle Builders. At the library, research several physical fitness books to learn how to build the **deltoids** and the **quadriceps**. Then give a five-minute speech and demonstration on how to build these two sets of muscles. In your talk, explain what the two sets of muscles do and which sports they are used in.

Name ______________________________ Date ______________

Body Terms

Read each brief description below. Circle the word in each row that matches the description or definition. You may use a dictionary.

1. carries blood away from heart	**esophagus**	**artery**	**vein**
2. strong, muscular tube connecting throat to stomach	**esophagus**	**melanin**	**diaphragm**
3. tough, fibrous connective tissue attached to bones	**cartilage**	**epiglottis**	**marrow**
4. minute blood vessels that connect arteries and veins	**sinuses**	**capillaries**	**esophagus**
5. closes over the windpipe each time you swallow	**lymph**	**diaphragm**	**epiglottis**
6. dark pigment present in skin, hair, retina	**lymph**	**artery**	**melanin**
7. fat and blood cells in natural bone cavities	**epiglottis**	**marrow**	**vein**
8. air-filled cavities in the cranial bones	**capillaries**	**cartilage**	**sinuses**
9. clear fluid that contains white blood cells	**lymph**	**melanin**	**epiglottis**
10. strong sheet of muscles that controls breathing	**melanin**	**esophagus**	**diaphragm**

Artery Comparison Look up the word *artery* in a dictionary. On a separate sheet of paper, write two paragraphs on the similarities and differences between blood arteries and traffic arteries.

Name ______________________________ Date ______________

Call the Doctor

Each boldfaced word below names an illness. Read each question, then circle the word that is the answer. On the line below each term, define the word that you did *not* circle. You may use a dictionary.

1. Is an inflammation of a nerve or nerves called **neuritis** or **epilepsy**?

   ____

2. A **cataract** or a **sty**—which is an acute infection of one of the tiny glands in the eyelid?

   ____

3. When the blood supply to the brain is cut off, is the result a **shock** or a **stroke**?

   ____

4. Is an inflammation of the mucous lining of the stomach called **gastritis** or **colitis**?

   ____

5. **Cystitis** or **hepatitis**—which is an inflammation of the liver?

   ____

6. Is pain in the lower back called **lumbago** or **bursitis**?

   ____

7. Is a large bump on the big toe joint a **wart** or a **bunion**?

   ____

8. **Psoriasis** or **neuralgia**—which is a skin disease that leaves the skin bleeding and itchy?

   ____

9. **Anemia** or **hemophilia**—which is a condition in which the blood contains fewer than the normal number of red blood cells?

   ____

10. Is the medical name for lockjaw **tetanus** or **diphtheria**?

    ____

More Problems On a separate sheet of paper, define each of the following diseases or conditions: **asthma, conjunctivitis, diabetes, gingivitis, gout, meningitis, pleurisy, pneumonia, sciatica, trachoma.**

Name ______________________________ Date ______________

Medical Terms Word Wheel

The word wheel below contains ten medical terms. Separate the letters into ten words. Then write each of the ten words on the line next to its correct definition.

anestheticprosthesiscomatoseintravenoussymptomtherapeuticneurosisdetoxifycarcinogenmalinger

______________ 1. something that causes total or partial loss of the sense of pain

______________ 2. a sign or indication of something

______________ 3. a substance that causes cancer

______________ 4. an artificial substitute for a missing body part

______________ 5. a mental functional disorder

______________ 6. helping to heal or cure

______________ 7. to pretend to be ill

______________ 8. directly in or into a vein

______________ 9. to remove a poison from

______________ 10. in a coma or stupor

Fictional Farce On a separate sheet of paper, write a short story entitled "Malbert the Malingerer."

Name ________________________________ Date ______________

Houses Around the World

Cabin, castle, chalet, duplex, hogan, igloo, longhouse, pagoda, pueblo, tepee, wigwam, yurt – each of these houses or building types is defined and pictured below. Write the correct letter under each picture; then write the correct vocabulary word under each picture. You may use a dictionary.

A. dwelling with gently sloping overhanging roof, common in Switzerland
B. circular, domed portable tent used by nomadic Mongols
C. community dwelling built of stone or adobe by Southwest Indian tribes
D. apartment with rooms on two adjoining floors
E. small, roughly built house
F. long, wooden Iroquois dwelling
G. cone-shaped tent of skins or bark
H. Eskimo dwelling, sometimes built of blocks of snow or ice
I. structure built in imitation of far Eastern religious buildings
J. earth-covered Navaho dwelling
K. North American Indian dwelling with arched frame overlaid with bark or hides
L. a fortified stronghold used as a residence

1. ___ ______________ 2. ___ ______________ 3. ___ ______________

4. ___ ______________ 5. ___ ______________ 6. ___ ______________

7. ___ ______________ 8. ___ ______________ 9. ___ ______________

10. ___ ______________ 11. ___ ______________ 12. ___ ______________

Gimme Shelter Read a book on survival in the wilderness. On a separate sheet of paper, write three paragraphs that explain how to construct a shelter in the wilderness.

Name ______________________________ Date ______________

Castles on the Ground

All the words below have to do with castles. Write the letter of each term next to its correct definition. You may use a dictionary.

_______ 1. a fortified group of buildings that dominates the surrounding country

_______ 2. the stronghold (jail) of a castle

_______ 3. a wide, deep ditch surrounding a castle as protection against assault

_______ 4. the outer wall of a castle

_______ 5. a defensive fence of pointed stakes

_______ 6. a room where food, china, and silverware were kept

_______ 7. an underground vault used as a burial place

_______ 8. an exceptionally tall part of a building

_______ 9. communal toilet, usually without plumbing

_______ 10. embankment that served as fortification against attack

_______ 11. a small rear gate of a castle

_______ 12. a sliding grill of iron suspended in a large gate—it could be lowered quickly in case of attack

a. **palisade**

b. **bailey**

c. **rampart**

d. **crypt**

e. **portcullis**

f. **castle**

g. **pantry**

h. **latrine**

i. **postern**

j. **keep**

k. **tower**

l. **moat**

Tapestry The interior walls of many castles were hung with tapestry. Use library resources to read about tapestry. On a separate sheet of paper, write a report on the history of tapestry.

Name ______________________________ Date ______________

Hidden Materials

From the earliest times, certain natural materials have been used to construct shelters. **Reeds** constituted an early shelter material, as did **skin** (animal hides). **Clay** and **adobe** (sun-dried, unbaked clay bricks) were also early building materials. **Wood** was and still is used in many forms, including **logs**, **shingles**, and **clapboard**. **Stone** was often used to build a solid house. In some places, **sod** was used. **Pozzuolana**, which is volcanic ash, is still used as a building material in some places. **Concrete** is also a building material, as is **stucco**, which is used as either an interior or exterior finish.

The names of the thirteen boldfaced building materials are hidden in the puzzle below. The words run from left to right or from top to bottom. Circle each of the thirteen words. Then list each word below in its correct category. You may use a dictionary.

A B C D E J I H W O B O J I Z A R O F T

U V S K I N W S P Q R A B K L M L N O F

G H I J E P J O O B W O R V A N O I D C

H E M R O O X D E A Z T S H I N G L E S

C Q L G B Z E A F S P A K S I B S G L E

L C H E D Z I N W O O D Z Z N O B A E R

A A S I D U P F K G L O I E H M I N J O

Y D I J E O C H D I B B G S T O N E F A

S P R O Q L T R U V A E B W O B N A M R

K P E L Q A S T R I Z A R Z S T U C C O

W V E U T N S B A C L A P B O A R D R D

A B D E J A C O N C R E T E O D N I M H

C P S S T A B G C H D I Z J B O W O V Z

Materials from Plants: ______________ ______________ ______________

______________ ______________

Materials from Earth (Dirt): ______________ ______________ ______________

Materials from Animals: ______________

Materials from Minerals: ______________ ______________ ______________

____

Cement or Concrete? People often misuse the terms ***cement*** and ***concrete***. What is the difference between the two? On the back of this sheet of paper, write a definition of each term. Then write a slogan or motto that will help people remember the difference.

Name ________________________________ Date ____________

Stairway to Words

Next to each part of the stairway diagram below, write the correct vocabulary word. Then complete each definition of the four extra words below. You may use a dictionary.

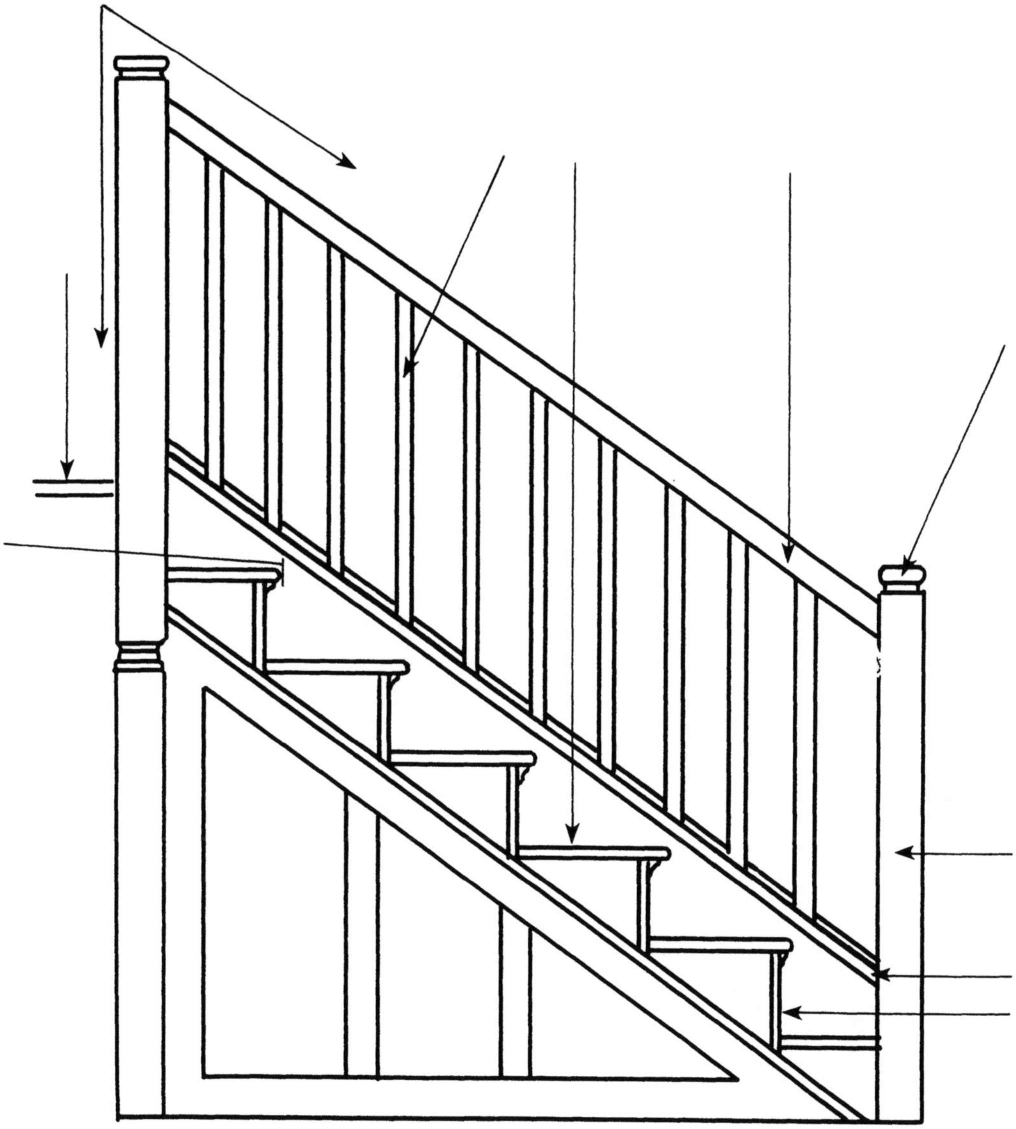

balustrade
baluster
banister
bottom rail
landing
newel cap
newel post
nosing
riser
tread

A **step** is a ________________________________

Stairs are ________________________________

A **staircase** is a ________________________________

A **stairwell** is a ________________________________

Escalator Words Number a separate sheet of paper from 1 to 30. Make as many smaller words as you can out of the word *escalator*. (There are at least thirty words; list more than thirty if you can.)

Name ________________________________ Date ________________

Houses Galore!

Read the following ad. In the space provided below, write a definition for each boldfaced word. You may use a dictionary.

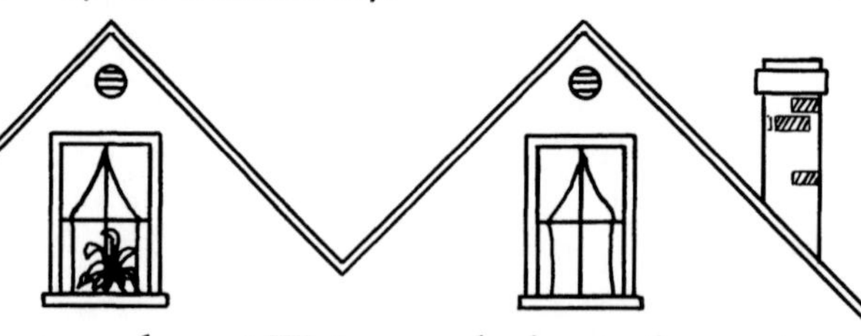

You want a house? We've got the house for you!
You name it, we've got it!
Feeling elegant? Perhaps a **townhouse** tucked away on a spiffy street
will suit you—or a **condominium** on a cul-de-sac.
Feeling rustic? Maybe a **saltbox** or an old **Cape Cod cottage**
is what you want. We've got a **bungalow**, too!
Is suburban what you want?
Then how about a **ranch house**, or a **split-level house**?
Maybe you're a handy person? Carpentry skills?
Want to remodel an old **duplex**?
Or how about an entire **tenement**? Now that's a challenge!
Feel like taking off? We've got **mobile homes**.
Futuristic? How about a **solar house**?
Uncluttered? How about an **A-frame**?
You name it, we've got it—houses galore!

1. ________________________________
2. ________________________________
3. ________________________________
4. ________________________________
5. ________________________________
6. ________________________________
7. ________________________________
8. ________________________________
9. ________________________________
10. ________________________________
11. ________________________________
12. ________________________________

Dream House Blueprint If you were to design a house or apartment to live in, what would it look like? Draw a floorplan of the kind of house or apartment you would like to live in.

Name ______________________________ Date ______________

Architecture Blanks

Fill in the blanks below by writing the correct word on each line. You may use your dictionary.

post	apse	lintel	capital	column
arch	dome	vault	buttress	rotunda

1. The ______________________ is a horizontal beam across two supporting columns.
2. An arched structure that forms a ceiling or roof is called a(n) ______________________ .
3. A(n) ______________________ is a circular building, usually with a dome.
4. The ______________________ is an upright beam.
5. A brick or stone structure built against a wall, the ______________________ gives the wall additional support.
6. A hemispherical vault is called a(n) ______________________ .
7. The ______________________ is a supporting pillar that consists of a base, a shaft, and a capital.
8. A(n) ______________________ is a semicircular projection (usually with a dome) at the end of a building.
9. The ______________________ is a structural device forming the curved edge of an opening.
10. The top part of a column is called the ______________________ .

Wren Report At the library, read about Christopher Wren. Write a two-page report telling about his life and achievements.

Name ______________________________ Date ______________

Household Words

Casement, jamb, knob, linoleum, parquet, sash, sill, skylight, terrazzo, threshold – each of these vocabulary words refers to a part of or kind of window, door, or floor. First define the three main terms below. Then write each of the ten vocabulary words under its correct category, and write a definition of each vocabulary word. (A few words may fit more than one category: you may put them into either category.) You may use a dictionary.

1. A **window** is ______________________________

   Window words are:

   a. ______________ ______________________________

   b. ______________ ______________________________

   c. ______________ ______________________________

   d. ______________ ______________________________

2. A **door** is ______________________________

   Door words are:

   a. ______________ ______________________________

   b. ______________ ______________________________

   c. ______________ ______________________________

3. A **floor** is ______________________________

   Floor words are:

   a. ______________ ______________________________

   b. ______________ ______________________________

   c. ______________ ______________________________

Porch Terms On a separate sheet of paper, define each of these words: **deck, patio, piazza, porch, stoop, terrace, veranda.**

Name ______________________________ Date ______________

Roof Styles

Dome, flat, gable, gambrel, hip, lean-to, mansard, pyramid, saltbox – these are all roof styles. Write the correct term under each illustration below. You may use the dictionary.

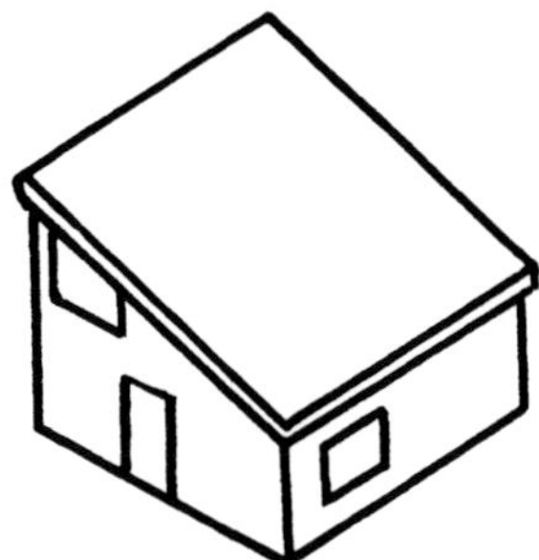

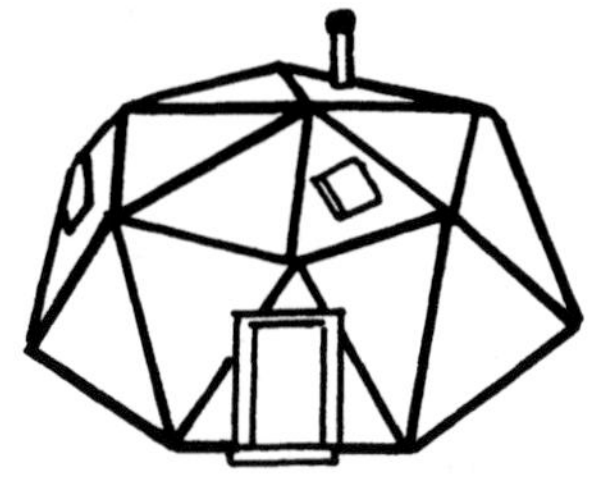

1. ______________ 2. ______________ 3. ______________

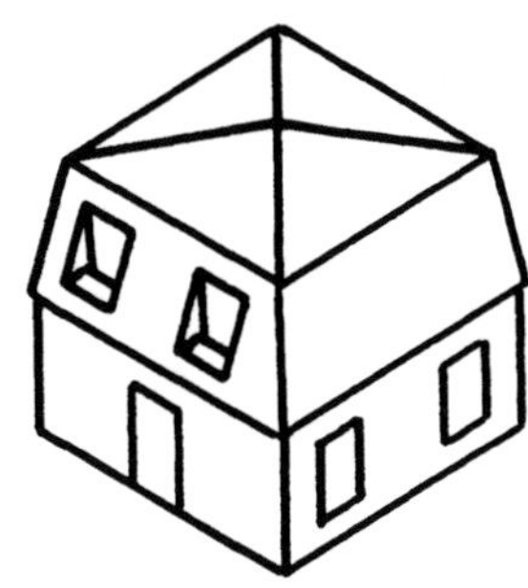

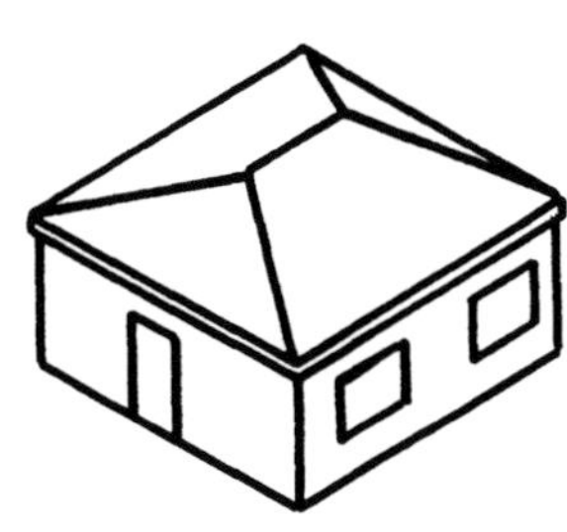

4. ______________ 5. ______________ 6. ______________

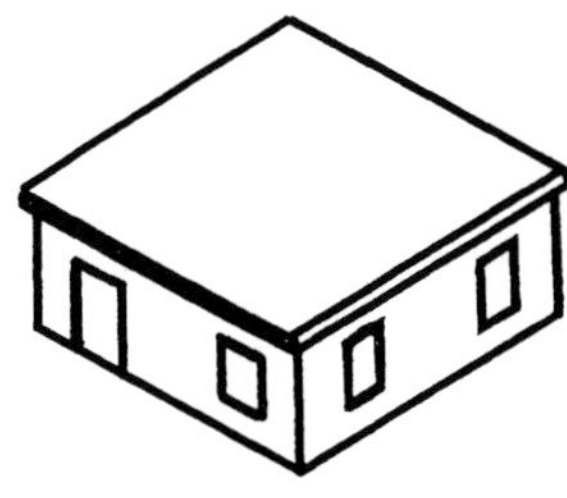

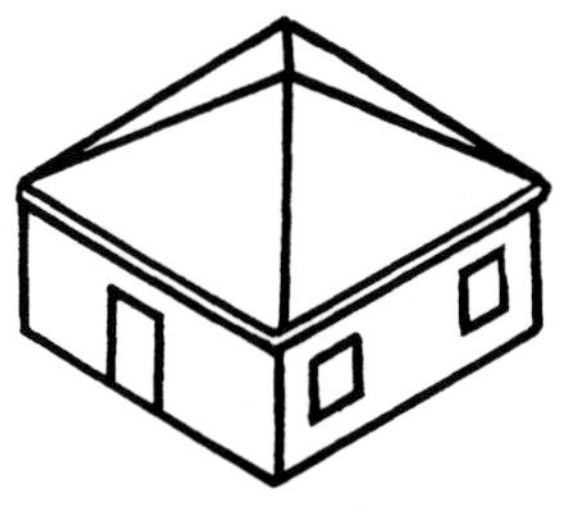

7. ______________ 8. ______________ 9. ______________

Roof* to *Card* in Ten Steps** You can change the word ***roof into the word ***card*** in ten steps by changing one letter each time. It goes like this: *roof, hoof, hoot, soot, sort, fort, fork, cork, cord, card.* What other word or words can you change ***roof*** into in ten steps? Number the back of this sheet of paper from 1–10. Write ***roof*** on the first line. Then begin! (*Hint:* you can change ***roof*** into *poof, goof, woof, rook,* or *rood.*)

Name ______________________________ Date ______________

Real Estate Terms

p r i n c i p a l m o r t g a g e l i e n e a r n e s t i n t e r e s t

There are ten words in the letters at the top and bottom of this page. Separate the letters into words. Then write the correct word on each line below. You may use a dictionary.

1. ______________________ is a charge (usually a percentage) on borrowed money.
2. The right to ownership of real estate is called a(n) ______________________.
3. ______________________ is a deed, bond, money, or piece of property put in the care of a third party.
4. The ______________________ is the amount of a debt minus the interest and other charges.
5. A(n) ______________________ is an expert valuation of a house for the purposes of selling it.
6. Paid to the real estate agent, the ______________________ is a percentage of the selling price of a piece of property.
7. ______________________ is money given as a partial payment and as a pledge in binding a bargain.
8. A(n) ______________________ is the pledging of property to a creditor. It acts as security for the payment of the debt.
9. A sum of money lent (usually for a specified period of time, usually to be repaid with interest) is called a(n) ______________________.
10. A(n) ______________________ is a claim on property as security for payment of a debt.

c o m m i s s i o n t i t l e a p p r a i s a l l o a n e s c r o w

Yancey the Younger Look up the word ***primogeniture***. Then, on a separate sheet of paper, write a fictional story about Yancey, the younger son of an aristocratic British family of 1760. The plot of your story should include the fact of primogeniture and Yancey's feelings and actions in regard to it.

Name ______________________________ Date ______________

More Architecture

Arcade, atrium, auditorium, balcony, basilica, belvedere, cantilever, chamber, clerestory, courtyard, dormitory, foyer, gallery, hall, lobby, parapet, vestibule – twelve of these seventeen words fit one of the definitions below. Write each word on the correct line. You may use a dictionary.

1. _ **a** _ _
2. _ _ **r** _ _ _
3. **c** _ _ _ _ _ _ _ _ _
4. _ **h** _ _ _ _ _
5. _ _ _ **i** _ _ _ _
6. _ _ _ **t** _ _ _ _ _
7. _ _ _ _ **e** _ _ _ _
8. _ _ _ **c** _ _ _
9. _ _ _ _ _ _ **t** _ _ _
10. _ _ **u** _ _ _ _ _ _
11. _ **r** _ _ _ _
12. _ _ _ _ **e** _ _

1. the great central room in a large dwelling; a passageway from an entrance to the interior
2. the central court of an ancient Roman house; an entrance court
3. a large block or beam projecting from a wall
4. a room in a house
5. a rectangular building ending in an apse, often used as a courtroom or public hall
6. a small entrance hall
7. a structure such as a balcony or gallery that commands a beautiful view
8. a platform that projects from the wall of a building and is surrounding by a railing of some kind
9. a windowed wall used for light and ventilation
10. an open space surrounded by walls or buildings
11. a series of arches supported by columns; an arched, roofed building
12. a roofed promenade extending along the wall of a building

Mall Meaning On a separate sheet of paper, write three paragraphs in which you do the following: (a) define a mall; (b) discuss what purpose malls serve; (c) discuss what conditions must exist for a mall to be successful.

Name ______________________________ Date ______________

City Terms

Each vocabulary word or term below has been divided into two parts. The first part is in Column 1 and the second part is in Column 2. Put the word parts together correctly. Then write the correct word next to each brief definition or description. You may use a dictionary.

		1	2
______________	1. residential community just outside a city	**bar**	**to**
______________	2. a very tall building	**inner**	**lord**
______________	3. older, central part of a city	**ghet**	**urb**
______________	4. a Spanish-speaking neighborhood in a U.S. city	**gentri**	**scraper**
______________	5. the restoration of deteriorated urban property	**slum**	**ral**
______________	6. a person who specializes in city problems	**urban**	**city**
______________	7. slum section of a city occupied by a minority group	**sub**	**ologist**
______________	8. a landlord of poor housing in an urban area	**urban**	**rio**
______________	9. the process of making something citylike	**sky**	**fication**
______________	10. referring to the country as opposed to the city	**ru**	**ization**

City Cousin and Country Cousin On a separate sheet of paper, write a story in which Country Cousin visits City Cousin. Create a situation in which both the advantages and disadvantages of city living are highlighted.

Name ______________________________ Date ______________

Clothes Crossword

Solve the crossword puzzle by writing the correct word in each blank. You may use a dictionary.

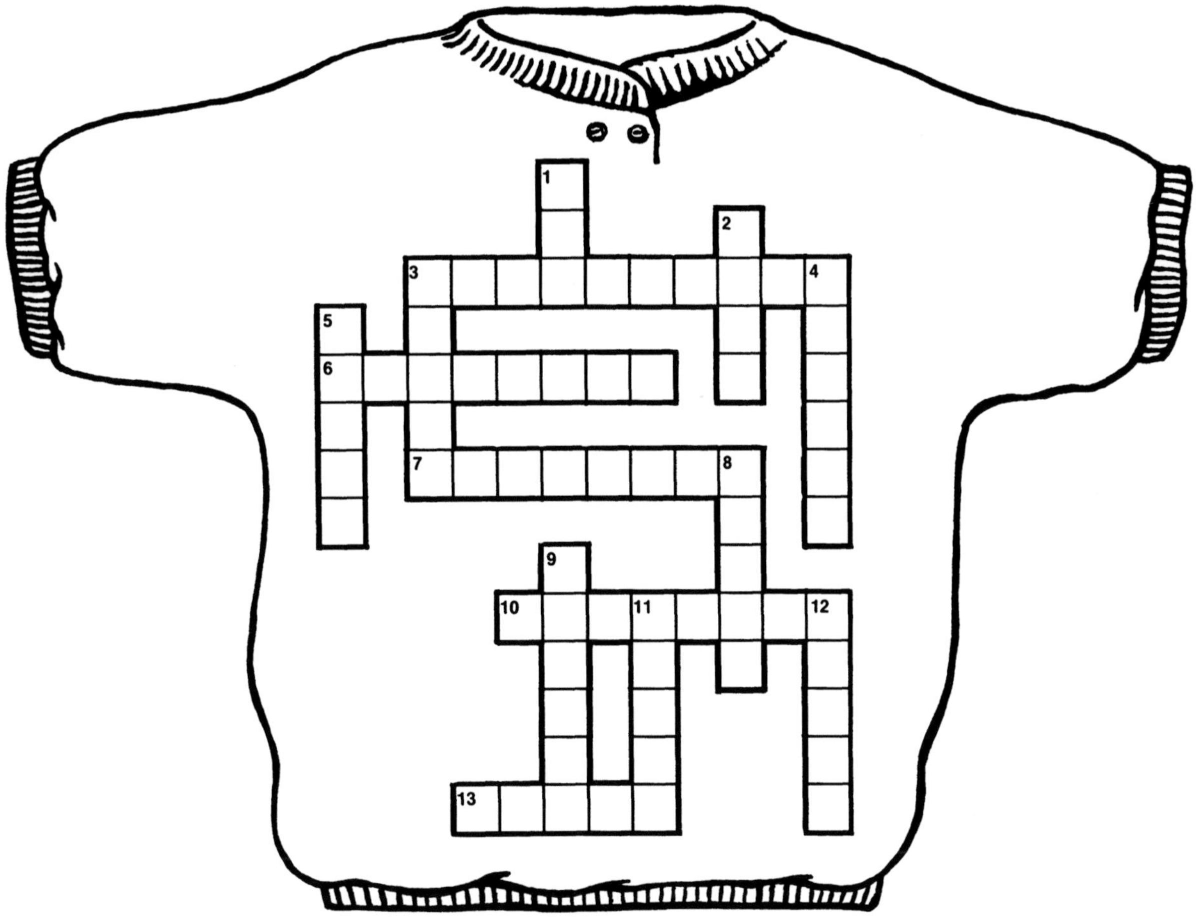

Across

3. supporting bands worn across the shoulders to hold up skirts or pants
6. short pants, loose-fitting, gathered at the knees
7. another word for 11 Down
10. light, low-cut shoes
13. outer garment that is a one-piece bodice and skirt

Down

1. head covering without a brim
2. strip of material worn around the waist
3. a garment with collar, sleeves, and a front opening for the upper part of the body
4. very short pants
5. free-hanging outer garment extending from the waist down
8. outer coverings for the feet, usually made of leather
9. loose outer garment that covers the body from neck to waist
11. outer garment that covers each leg separately
12. knitted coverings for the feet

Trouser Research Today trousers are a common item of wear in the western and eastern worlds. What did people in the western world wear in medieval times in place of trousers? Find this information in the library. Then write a two-page report on the history of clothing that led up to the wearing of trousers.

Name ______________________________ Date ______________

Shoe Types

Define each of the three boldfaced numbered terms below. Then write each of the boldfaced words from the list under the proper category. You may use a dictionary.

1. **Shoes** are ______________________________
____
____

Examples of types of shoes are: ______________
____
____
____

2. **Sandals** are ______________________________
____
____

Examples of types of sandals are: ______________
____
____
____

3. **Boots** are ______________________________
____
____

Examples of types of boots are: ______________
____
____
____

4. Examples of nonshoe leg coverings are: ______________
____
____
____

bluchers

brogans

buskins

chukkas

espadrilles

gillies

huaraches

jodhpurs

mukluks

mules

oxfords

pumps

puttees

spats

thongs

Wellingtons

zoris

Shoe Draw Choose one example from each of the four categories above. On a separate sheet of paper, draw a picture of each example. Label each of the four drawings.

Name ______________________________ Date ______________

Fabric Sounds

Each fabric word below is spelled the way it sounds. (Dictionaries give these phonetic spellings after each word.) After each phonetic spelling, write the actual spelling of the word. Then write the letter of the correct definition in front of each word. You may use a dictionary.

______ 1. **rā än** _ _ _ _ _

______ 2. **kät n** _ _ _ _ _ _

______ 3. **silk** _ _ _ _

______ 4. **rā mē** _ _ _ _ _

______ 5. **wu̇l** _ _ _ _

______ 6. **lin ən** _ _ _ _ _

______ 7. **sī səl** _ _ _ _ _

______ 8. **felt** _ _ _ _

______ 9. **nī län** _ _ _ _ _

______ 10. **raf ē ə** _ _ _ _ _ _

______ 11. **ə kril ik** _ _ _ _ _ _ _

______ 12. **or län** _ _ _ _ _

a. a soft, curly fiber from various hairy mammals

b. a smooth fiber made from cellulose materials

c. the fiber of a palm, used in making baskets and hats

d. cloth made of a mixture of wool, fur, and other fibers pressed together through heat, moisture, and chemicals

e. the strong, lustrous fiber from an Asian plant (*Boehmeria*) of the nettle family

f. thread, yarn, or cloth made from the flax plant

g. a lustrous, tough protein fiber produced by insect larvae

h. an elastic synthetic material used for fiber, filaments, and bristles

i. the strong white fiber from agave leaves, used for cordage and twine

j. a soft white fiber composed of the hairs around the seeds of the plant *Gossypium* of the mallow family

k. a trademark used for an acrylic fiber

l. a quick-drying synthetic fiber made of acrylonitrile

Fiber List On a separate sheet of paper label one column Synthetic Fibers and the other Natural Fibers. Try to list at least ten examples of each type of fiber.

Name ______________________ Date ______________

Hats Off!

Each picture on the left illustrates a type of head covering. The name of each is next to the picture, scrambled. Unscramble each word and write it on the correct line. You may use a dictionary.

byred 1. ______________

doho 2. ______________

tranub 3. ______________

cholec 4. ______________

treeb 5. ______________

adofer 6. ______________

shukabab 7. ______________

atrobe 8. ______________

treedslarke 9. ______________

bomerros 10. ______________

mat 11. ______________

notneb 12. ______________

Why a Hat? On a separate sheet of paper, write a two-paragraph essay giving your opinion on why most people (both men and women) wore hats up until the very recent past, and why few people seem to wear hats today.

Name ______________________________ Date ______________

Proper Clothes

Write an answer to each question below. You may use a dictionary.

1. Named after the Earl of Chesterfield in the 1850s, the piece of clothing known as a **chesterfield** is ______________________________
____

2. Because it first came from Damascus, it was called damask. **Damask** is ______________
____
____

3. Named after Inverness, Scotland, an **inverness** is ______________________________
____

4. Invented by the trapeze artist Jules Leotard, it is of course called a leotard. A **leotard** is
____

5. Invented by Levi Strauss when he went to California to look for gold, they are called Levi's. **Levi's** are ______________________________
____

6. Named after Charles Mackintosh, who invented it, a **mackintosh** is ______________
____

7. In the 1790s Lord Spencer said that fashion was so absurd that even he could wear something different and make it into a new style. He altered an item of his clothing and set the style. A **spencer** is a ______________________________
____

8. In the play based on George du Maurier's novel *Trilby*, a new fashion was inspired. A **trilby** is ______________________________
____

9. Baron Raglan wanted ease of movement above all. So his tailor designed the **raglan sleeve**, which is ______________________________
____

10. Named after the seventh Earl of Cardigan, a **cardigan is** ______________________________
____

Clothing Future On a separate sheet of paper, label one column Similar and another Dissimilar. Then list at least six ways in which clothing a hundred years from now will probably be similar to today's and six ways in which it will probably be dissimilar.

Name ______________________________ Date ______________

Outer Coverings

Read each definition on the left-hand side. Circle the one word from the three boldfaced words that best matches the definition. You may use a dictionary.

1. same as a parka	**anorak**	**cardigan**	**mackinaw**
2. a long cotton jacket with four pockets and a belt	**mess jacket**	**bush jacket**	**dress jacket**
3. sleeveless covering fastened at the neck—it hangs loosely	**cloak**	**pullover**	**cape**
4. blanket-like covering with hole in center for wearer's head	**poncho**	**mackinaw**	**parka**
5. double-breasted short coat of heavy wool plaid cloth	**mackinaw**	**pea jacket**	**anorak**
6. loose, sleeveless coat	**cloak**	**anorak**	**parka**
7. loose-fitting belted jacket with box pleats	**trench coat**	**Norfolk jacket**	**pea jacket**
8. hip-length pullover coat with a hood	**pullover**	**parka**	**cloak**
9. belted raincoat with military-type shoulder straps	**mackinaw**	**trench coat**	**kersey**
10. sweater that has neither buttons nor zippers	**anorak**	**poncho**	**pullover**
11. short, tight-fitting, sleeveless covering worn under jacket	**cape**	**vest**	**pea jacket**
12. hip-length double-breasted coat of heavy wool	**cloak**	**trench coat**	**pea jacket**

The Needle One of the most important inventions of early times was the needle. On the back of this sheet of paper, write two paragraphs explaining the importance of the needle.

Name ______________________________ Date ______________

Textile Differences

Write an answer to each question below. You may use the dictionary.

1. What is the difference between **thread** and **yard**? ______________

____

____

2. What is the difference between **nap** and **pile**? ______________

____

____

3. How are **hemp** and **coir** similar? ______________

____

____

4. What is the relationship between **twill** and **tweed**? ______________

____

____

5. What is the difference between **cambric** and **poplin**? ______________

____

____

6. What is **mercerized** thread? ______________

____

____

7. How do **sewing** and **weaving** differ? ______________

____

____

8. How does **damask** differ from **velvet**? ______________

____

____

Fabric and Patterns On a separate sheet of paper, define the following words: **argyle, foulard, jacquard, seersucker, serge, taffeta, tattersall.**

Name ______________________________ Date ______________

Shoe Terms

Study the diagram below. Write the correct vocabulary word on each line of the diagram. You may use a dictionary.

aglet **counter** **eyelet** **heel** **instep** **lining** **quarter**

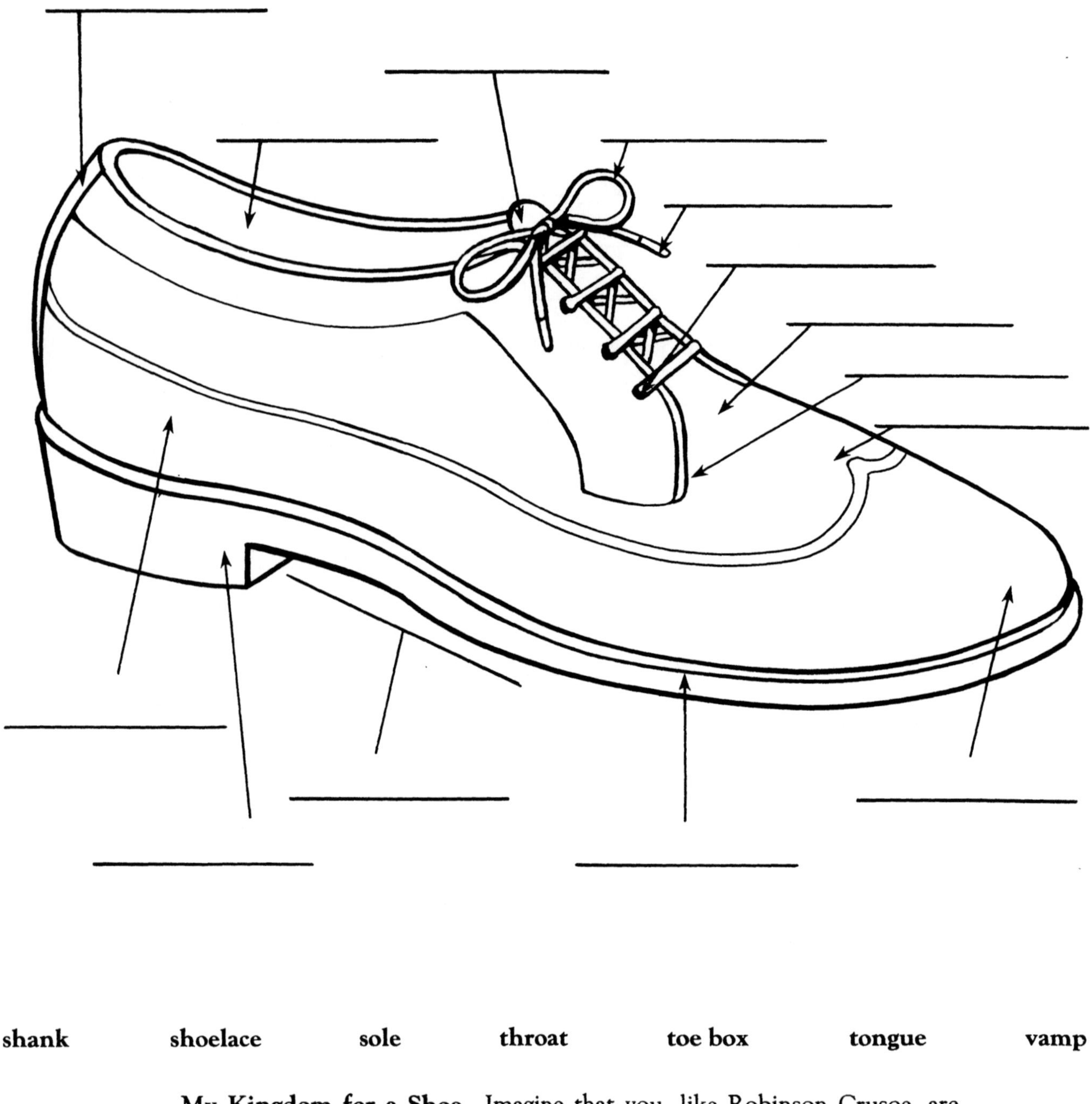

shank **shoelace** **sole** **throat** **toe box** **tongue** **vamp**

My Kingdom for a Shoe Imagine that you, like Robinson Crusoe, are stranded on a deserted island. You must make your own clothing and your own footwear. What kind of footwear could you make? On a separate sheet of paper, write numbered instructions explaining how you would go about making footwear.

Name ______________________________ Date ______________

Clothing Museum

Read the story below. Replace each boldfaced definition with the correct vocabulary word. You may use the dictionary.

bodice	**stomacher**	**ruff**	**jerkin**	**baldric**
pelisse	**redingote**	**fichu**	**doublet**	**reticule**

"Now there," said the museum guide, "is a handsome gentleman dressed in a ____________________ (**double-breasted coat with a cape and revers**). Next to him, however, is a model wearing a much earlier style of adornment: a ____________________ (**wide silk sash worn over the right shoulder**). He is being stared at by the young woman about to be helped into the carriage. She is wearing a ____________________ (**full-length, long-sleeved cloak or robe lined with fur**)."

Moving down another aisle, the museum guide continued her lecture. "There stands a man wearing a ____________________ (**short, close-fitting sleeveless coat of leather**). It is also known as a ____________________ . Such an item of clothing was no doubt fairly comfortable. What must have been most uncomfortable is exhibited on the female model to your left. Notice the tight ____________________ (**part of the dress above the waist**) and the ____________________ (**separate front panel that ends in a deep point**)".

"Now please notice that **stiffly starched collar that encircles the neck.** It's called a ____________________ . You have probably seen a portrait of Shakespeare wearing one. If you look at the female model across the aisle, however, you'll note that she is wearing a ____________________ (**a neck cloth draped over the shoulders of a gown**). The model next to that one, please note, is carrying a ____________________ (**small handbag**). I wonder whether any of these styles will ever return to fashion?"

Thoreau on Clothes Read "Economy," the first chapter of *Walden* by Henry David Thoreau. Write a three-page report on what Thoreau had to say about clothing in this chapter.

Name ______________________________ Date ______________

Clothes of the World

Bolero, caftan, dhoti, kilt, kimono, muu muu, obi, rebozo, sabot, sari, sarong, serape – these are all clothing items from around the world. Write the correct term under each illustration below. You may use a dictionary.

1. ______________ 2. ______________ 3. ______________

4. ______________ 5. ______________ 6. ______________

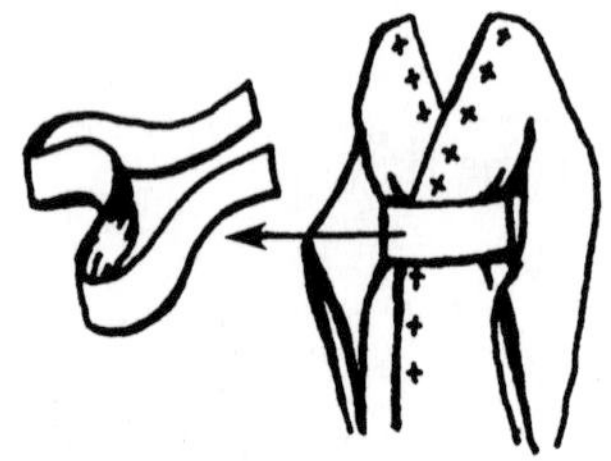
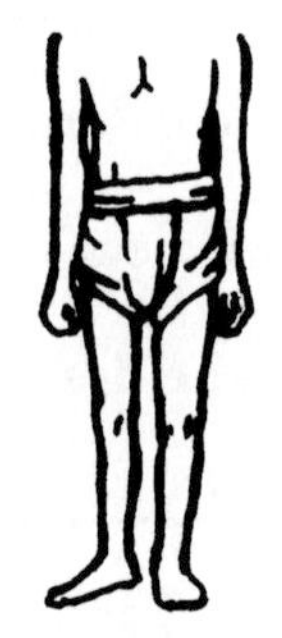

7. ______________ 8. ______________ 9. ______________

10. ______________ 11. ______________ 12. ______________

Pun Fun A pun is a play on words that sound the same. Choose two of the words above. On the back of this sheet of paper, write a pun (one or two sentences long) for each of the words.

Name ______________________________ Date ______________

Fashion Words

Read each brief definition or description on the left. Then fill in the correct word on the right. You may use a dictionary.

1. a tailor's dummy — **m _ _ _ _ q _ _ _**
2. stylish — **c _ _ _**
3. faddish — **t _ _ n _ _**
4. a brownish-gray color — **t a _ _ _**
5. a delicate purple color — **m _ _ _ e**
6. person who makes original patterns — **d _ _ _ _ n _ _**
7. a dark olive-green color — **l _ _ _ n**
8. the business of new fashion in women's clothes — **c o _ _ _ _ _ _**
9. adjective now meaning conservative, unimaginative — **b _ _ _ _ n-d _ _ n**
10. gathered — **s h _ _ _ _ _ _**
11. bell-bottomed — **f _ _ _ _ e _**
12. a dark red — **p _ _ _**
13. initialed — **m _ _ _ g _ _ m _ _ _**
14. separate articles of clothing designed to go together — **c _ o _ _ _ _ n _ _ _ _**
15. a dark greenish-blue — **t _ _ _**

Color Wheel Read about color in an encyclopedia or reference book. Then make a chart in the form of a wheel or square showing the families of colors and the names for various colors.

Name ______________________ Date ______________

What Is It?

Read each definition or description below. Circle the letter of the correct answer. You may use a dictionary.

1. A loose-fitting, brightly colored tunic modeled after an African garment
   (a) **balaclava** (b) **madras** (c) **dashiki**
2. An Oriental-style high-necked dress with a slit partway up the side
   (a) **cheongsam** (b) **grenadine** (c) **pongee**
3. A dress with a full skirt, a close-fitting bodice, and a gathered waist
   (a) **froufrou** (b) **buckram** (c) **dirndl**
4. A one-piece woman's swimsuit
   (a) **manta** (b) **maillot** (c) **melton**
5. A sturdy, closely woven cotton fabric
   (a) **russet** (b) **lawn** (c) **duck**
6. A sleeveless apronlike dress worn over a dress or blouse
   (a) **bombazine** (b) **wraparound** (c) **pinafore**
7. A loose blouse with a sailor collar
   (a) **pantaloon** (b) **middy** (c) **kersey**
8. A loose, shirtlike covering worn to protect clothing
   (a) **mantilla** (b) **gusset** (c) **smock**
9. A woman's pair of pants that are short and full and resemble a skirt
   (a) **culottes** (b) **cutaways** (c) **tartans**
10. A woman's long scarf of feathers or fur worn around the neck or shoulders
    (a) **ascot** (b) **boa** (c) **bombazine**
11. A Canadian cap which is knitted and pointed at both ends and is worn by turning one end into the other.
    (a) **bateau** (b) **mobcap** (c) **tuque**
12. A lightweight single-breasted sports jacket in a solid color
    (a) **broadcloth** (b) **bush jacket** (c) **blazer**
13. A woven fabric, usually of cotton, with varied designs (often plaid) in bright colors
    (a) **madras** (b) **paisley** (c) **bombazine**
14. An insert in a seam to provide expansion or reinforcement
    (a) **bombazine** (b) **wraparound** (c) **gusset**
15. A scarf worn over the head and shoulders, especially by Spanish women
    (a) **dirndl** (b) **mantilla** (c) **boa**

The Sound of Clothes Close your eyes and imagine the sounds that different clothes make as people move. Can you imagine the sound of corduroy pants? Of leather boots? Of mittened hands? On the back of this sheet of paper, write a three-paragraph description of the sounds of different clothes.

Name ______________________ Date ______________

Which Road?

Seventeen words are hidden below. One of the words is ***road***. The other sixteen words are synonyms for ***road***. Circle each of the seventeen words. They run from left to right or from top to bottom. After you have circled all seventeen words, list them in alphabetical order in the space provided. You may use a dictionary.

T A F K O S X B G L P T R A C E T Y U Z

H C T U R N P I K E A P A T H H Q A U B

O D I M R V E E J N E W O E Z Y X S T S

R U V N R O A D E R Q P O K B L A P M W

O N H J T I V H T R A I L G O F A I B I

U C I D H E E F G H I J K L U A M K N T

G O G P R Q N P A R K W A Y L A N E R C

H E H S O T U V W X Y Z E O E W V U T H

F O W P U Q E R E S K L A M V N F G H B

A I A J G O W E N T J E E V A R M I D A

R C Y H H A Q U Z R Y T P L R G B A F C

E K O S W X E D C E B A J I D H G F N K

M A L K A E R Q P E S P L A N A D E O W

V U T S Y O E Z Y T X S O K L A M N E R

C R O U T E D E J I H G Y Z E V U T P A

Alphabetical Order

1. ______________
2. ______________
3. ______________
4. ______________
5. ______________
6. ______________
7. ______________
8. ______________
9. ______________
10. ______________
11. ______________
12. ______________
13. ______________
14. ______________
15. ______________
16. ______________
17. ______________

Road Poem Read Robert Frost's poem "The Road Not Taken." On a separate sheet of paper, write an analysis of what the poem means. Write one paragraph for each stanza of the poem.

Name ______________________________ Date ______________

Flying High

Fill in the blanks below by writing the correct word on each line. You may use the dictionary.

rocket	**blimp**	**kite**	**thrust**	**supersonic**
dirigible	**drone**	**drag**	**balloon**	**Mach number**

1. A ______________________ is a nonrigid, buoyant aircraft.
2. A pilotless aircraft operated by remote control is a ___________________ .
3. A light framework covered with cloth, paper, or plastic, a ______________________ climbs and flies in a steady breeze.
4. A ______________________ is a round, flexible bag inflated with a gas lighter than air, which causes it to rise and float.
5. The ratio of the speed of an object to the speed of sound is a ______________________ .
6. ___________________ is the slowing force exerted by air on a moving aircraft in flight.
7. A ______________________ is a device propelled by the ejection of matter such as gas.
8. Something that is ______________________ has a speed greater than the speed of sound.
9. A rigid, steerable, lighter-than-aircraft is a ______________________ .
10. ___________________ is the forward-directed force of a jet or rocket engine.

Kite Research At the library, research the subject of kites. Then write a two-page report on the history and uses of kites.

Name ______________________ Date ______________

Anchors Aweigh

Brig, catamaran, coracle, dory, dugout, galleon, kayak, outrigger, paddle boat, scull, skiff, trimaran – these are just a few of many different kinds of boats. Write the correct term under each illustration below. You may use a dictionary.

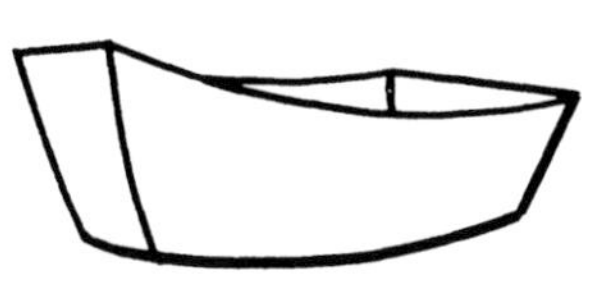

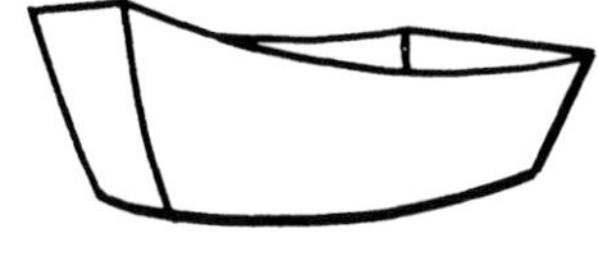

1. ______________ 2. ______________ 3. ______________

4. ______________ 5. ______________ 6. ______________

7. ______________ 8. ______________ 9. ______________

10. ______________ 11. ______________ 12. ______________

Pacific Adventure Read *Kon-Tiki*, by Thor Heyerdahl. Write a two-page summary of the book. Be certain to explain what Heyerdahl wanted to prove and how he set about doing it.

Name ______________________________ Date ______________

Going, Going, Gone

Read the auctioneer's words below. Then, on a separate sheet of paper, write each of the boldfaced words. Next to each word, write its definition. You may use a dictionary.

Driving men and driving women! What will you give me
for this little red **coupe**? Sold! – to the lady in the matching red coat!
What do I hear for this **sedan**?
Sold to the grandfather in the yellow suspenders!
And for this **fastback**?
Can you believe it, folks? – Sold to the little old lady from Pasadena!
Now what will you give me for this beautiful silver **hatchback**?
Sold! Sold to the lady in the flowered hat!
Next is this magnificant wood-paneled **station wagon**.
Sold! – to the gentleman holding the two babies!
What about this **limousine**, folks? Who'll take it?
Going, going, gone! — to the hombre in the cowboy hat!
Now there's a switch for you, folks!
Next we have a **van**. This one's a lovely lime-green model,
sure to stop traffic! Sold to. . . the gentleman holding the two babies!
Next comes a down-home model, folks—a **pickup truck**!
Sold! Sold to the lady in the red coat! My, my!
What about this **convertible**, folks?
Sold! – sold to the grandfather in the yellow suspenders!
Last of all is this **dune buggy**.
A beautiful, rugged monster of a dune buggy!
Sold! – to the little old lady from Pasadena!

Transportation Words Number a separate sheet of paper from 1 to 40. Make as many other words as you can out of the word ***transportation***. You should be able to make at least forty words. How far beyond forty can you go?

Name ______________________________ Date ______________

What's the Word?

Each brief definition or description below refers to a method of transportation. Write the word that goes with the definition in the spaces provided. You may use a dictionary.

1. public passenger car operated on rails through the streets of a city — _ _ _ e _ _ c _ _
2. vehicle with a metal frame mounted on two wheels, a seat, handlebars, and pedals — _ _ _ _ _ c _ _
3. two-wheeled vehicle of ancient times pulled by horses — _ _ a _ _ _ _
4. heavy automotive vehicle for transporting loads — _ _ _ _ _
5. child's vehicle with long footboard, two small wheels, and upright steering handle attached to front wheel — _ _ _ _ _ e _
6. long motor vehicle for carrying passengers — _ _ _
7. light, slender boat with pointed ends, moved by paddling — _ _ _ _ e
8. an elevated railroad for public transportation — _ _
9. four-wheeled, horse-drawn vehicle for private use and comfort — _ a _ _ _ _ _ e
10. boatlike vehicle with runners; sails on ice — _ _ e _ _ a _
11. string of connected cars pulled by locomotive on a track — _ _ _ _ _
12. small two-wheeled carriage pulled by one or two people; used in Orient — _ _ c _ _ _ a _
13. short, narrow board mounted on a set of four rollerskate wheels — _ _ a _ _ _ _ _ a _ _
14. underground urban railroad, usually run by electricity — _ _ _ _ a _
15. ship that can travel underneath the water — _ _ _ _ a _ _ _ e

Thirty Ways to Leave Number a separate sheet of paper from 1 to 10. Then label three columns: Land, Water, Air. List ten specific ways of traveling across each of these surfaces. (For example, under Water, a kayak would be one specific way of traveling.

Name ______________________________ Date ______________

True Sailing

Read each sentence below and think about the definition of the boldfaced word. Circle **T** if a statement is true. Circle **F** if it is false. If the sentence is false, write a correct definition of the boldfaced word on the back of this sheet of paper. You may use a dictionary.

T F 1. A ship's frames are attached to the **keel**, which runs lengthwise in a ship.

T F 2. A float moored in water to warn of danger or to serve as a marker is a **buoy**.

T F 3. A **spinnaker** is a wooden or metal pole used to support rigging.

T F 4. To **tack** is to bring a vessel into the wind in order to change the ropes that hold the course.

T F 5. The direction from which the wind blows is the **draft**.

T F 6. **Starboard** is the right-hand side of a ship as you face forward in the ship.

T F 7. **Leeward** refers to the side from which the wind is blowing.

T F 8. A person who specializes in the craft of making keels is a **keelson**.

T F 9. A rope used to lower or raise a sail is the **bulwarks**.

T F 10. A small crane used to hoist small boats, anchor, and cargo on a ship is a **davit**.

T F 11. A ship's **bow** consists of its lower deck.

T F 12. **Mooring** consists of the ropes that raise and lower sails.

T F 13. A ship's **stern** is its rear section.

T F 14. A **hatch** is an opening in a ship's deck.

T F 15. "All hands **astern**!" means that all hands should move toward the rear of the vessel.

Ship Drawing Draw a diagram of a sailing ship. Label its main parts.

Name ______________________________ Date ______________

Change a Letter

Each word on the left-hand side of the page has one incorrect letter in it. If you change the incorrect letter to the correct one, you will end up with a word that means to ***go*** or to ***move*** in a particular way. Change the wrong letter to a correct letter and write the vocabulary word in the space on the right. Then, on a separate sheet of paper, write twenty sentences: use one of the vocabulary words in each sentence. You may use a dictionary.

1. dread _ _ _ _ _
2. talk _ _ _ _
3. plot _ _ _ _
4. stripe _ _ _ _ _ _
5. stout _ _ _ _ _
6. coddle _ _ _ _ _ _
7. grudge _ _ _ _ _ _
8. tree _ _ _ _
9. migrane _ _ _ _ _ _ _
10. scroll _ _ _ _ _ _
11. tend _ _ _ _
12. rose _ _ _ _
13. growl _ _ _ _ _
14. stunter _ _ _ _ _ _ _
15. foam _ _ _ _
16. propenade _ _ _ _ _ _ _ _ _
17. marsh _ _ _ _ _
18. gamble _ _ _ _ _ _
19. dander _ _ _ _ _ _
20. mange _ _ _ _ _

Synonym Differences The English language is full of synonyms—words that have a similar meaning. But few words mean precisely the same as another word: there are usually shades of difference in the meaning. Choose five of the words above and, on a separate sheet of paper, explain the difference in meaning of the five words.

Name ______________________________ Date ______________

Bicycle Wheels

The word wheels below contain ten bicycle terms. Separate the letters into ten words. Then write each of the ten words on the line next to its correct definition.

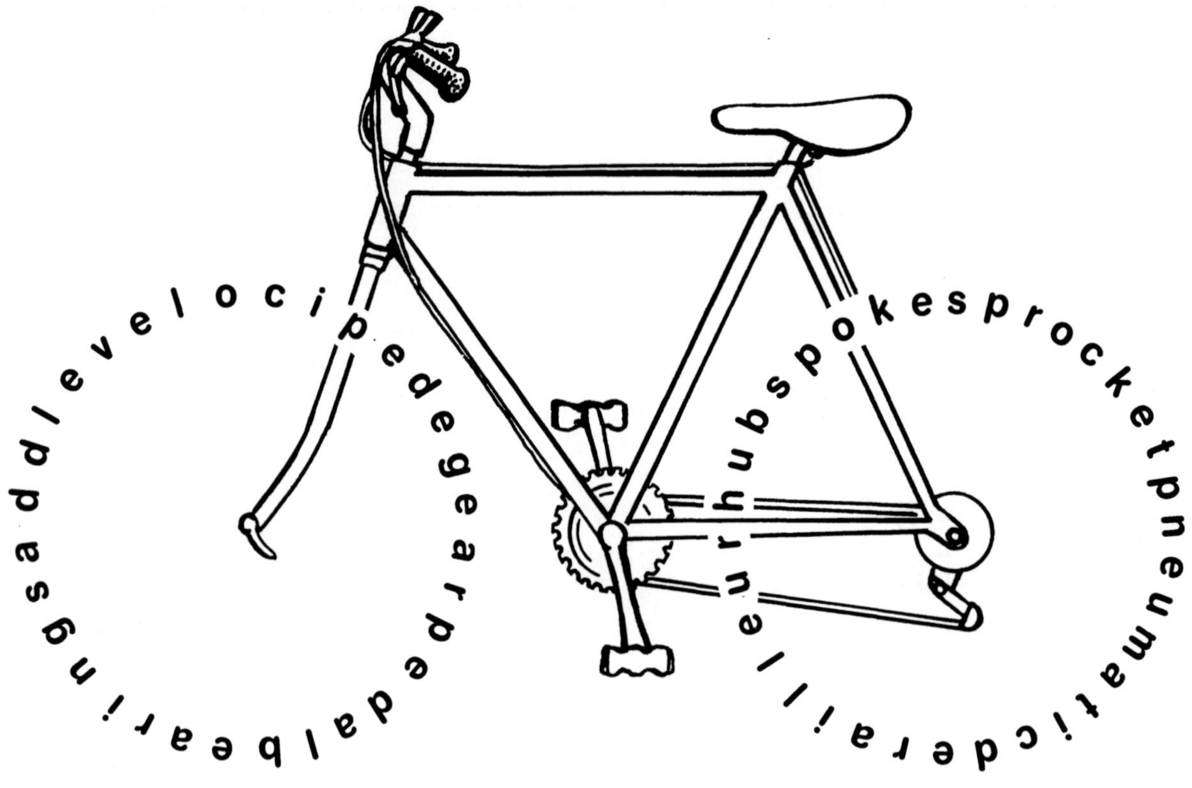

__________ 1. the seat of a bicycle

__________ 2. a machine lever worked by the foot

__________ 3. a toothed wheel in a machine that meshes with another to transmit motion and/or to change speed or direction

__________ 4. a toothlike projection on a wheel rim to engage the links of a chain

__________ 5. an early bicycle moved by pushing the feet along the ground while straddling the vehicle

__________ 6. the center portion of a wheel

__________ 7. a rod or brace that connects the wheel rim to the wheel center

__________ 8. a device that reduces the friction of motion between moving and fixed machine parts

__________ 9. filled with compressed air (as a tire)

__________ 10. a gear mechanism that changes gear ratio by moving the chain from one sprocket to another

"Help! Where Are the Brakes?" Did you know that early bicycles did not have brakes? On a separate sheet of paper, write a short story (set in the past) in which a bicyclist gets into trouble because there are no brakes on the bike.

Name ______________________________ Date ______________

Automatic Rhyme

Read each definition below. Write the answer on the line. The last syllable(s) of the answer rhymes with the boldfaced portion of the rhyme word. (Remember that words which rhyme are not always spelled similarly.) You may use a dictionary.

1. A machine that converts energy into mechanical motion.

   Rhymes with mar**lin**. _ _ _ _ _ _

2. A device for engaging (or disengaging) two working parts of a shaft.

   Rhymes with **Dutch**. _ _ _ _ _ _

3. An attachment for starting an internal combustion engine without hand cranking.
   Rhymes with **martyr**. _ _ _ _ _ _ _

4. A machine that converts mechanical energy into electrical energy.

   Rhymes with incu**bator**. _ _ _ _ _ _ _ _ _

5. A measure of a force's tendency to produce torsion and rotation about an axis.

   Rhymes with **cork**. _ _ _ _ _ _

6. A device that regulates the flow of gas or liquid through a structure by opening and closing.
   Rhymes with **salv**age. _ _ _ _ _

7. A device in a gasoline engine used to produce an efficient explosive vapor of fuel and air.
   Rhymes with vindi**cator**. _ _ _ _ _ _ _ _ _ _

8. The gearing mechanism of an engine that reduces power output required to maintain drive speed by increasing the ratio of the drive shaft to engine speed.

   Rhymes with sur**vive**. _ _ _ _ _ _ _ _ _

9. A device used in the internal-combustion engine to enrich the fuel mixture by reducing the flow of air to the carburetor.

   Rhymes with **smoke**. _ _ _ _ _

10. An automotive assembly of gears and associated parts by which power is transmitted from the engine to a driving axle.

    Rhymes with am**bition**. _ _ _ _ _ _ _ _ _ _ _ _

Car Songs Many, many songs have been written about cars. Choose two of these songs. Then write a two-page essay in which you compare the songs.

Name ______________________________ Date ______________

Railroad Compounds

Each railroad word on this page is a compound word—one word made out of two separate words (such as gold + fish = goldfish). Make the words for twelve railroad terms by combining one word from the left-hand car with one word from the right-hand car. Write each word on the correct line. You may use a dictionary.

hot	high	rail
box	tell	cow
cross	hand	round
piggy	road	fire

catcher	car	man
tie	road	bed
house	tale	car
back	ball	shot

__________ 1. a building for housing and switching locomotives

__________ 2. railroad signal indicating full speed ahead

__________ 3. person who stokes the engine

__________ 4. a nonstop freight train

__________ 5. a small, open railroad car moved by a hand pump or a small motor

__________ 6. a beam that connects and supports the rails of a railroad

__________ 7. road consisting of parallel steel rails

__________ 8. the foundation upon which the ties, rails, and ballast of a railroad are laid

__________ 9. a row of strips hung above a railroad track to warn an approaching train of a low clearance ahead

__________ 10. iron grill that projects from the front of a locomotive and clears the track of obstructions

__________ 11. method of transportation in which truck trailers are carried on trains

__________ 12. an enclosed and covered railroad car

Double Definitions Some of the compound words above have more than one definition. On the back of this sheet of paper, write five of the above words that have other definitions. Next to each word, write another (nonrailroad) definition for it.

Name ______________________________ Date ______________

Kitchen Jumble

Blender, cleaver, colander, grater, kettle, ricer, sieve, skewer, skillet, spatula, spoon, whisk – these words are scrambled below. Each one names a kitchen tool. Read each brief definition. Then unscramble the word and write it on the line. You may use a dictionary.

1. utensil of wire mesh used for straining or pureeing food	**eevis**	1. ______________
2. metal pot, with lid, for boiling or stewing	**letetk**	2. ______________
3. long metal pin used to secure or suspend food during cooking	**reswek**	3. ______________
4. bowl-shaped utensil for draining or rinsing foods	**dronalec**	4. ______________
5. tool with sharp-edged perforations on which to rub food to reduce it to shreds	**ragret**	5. ______________
6. pan for frying food	**liketls**	6. ______________
7. utensil for pushing soft food through small holes to reduce it to the size of small grain	**crire**	7. ______________
8. heavy, axlike knife	**vealcer**	8. ______________
9. utensil for whipping foods	**shikw**	9. ______________
10. electrical appliance with whirling blades for chopping or liquefying foods	**drelebn**	10. ______________
11. small tool with flat, flexible blade used to spread or lift foodstuffs	**atasupl**	11. ______________
12. small, shallow bowl on a handle, used in preparing, serving, or eating food	**opnos**	12. ______________

Kitchen Draw Choose six of the above kitchen tools to draw. On a separate sheet of paper, illustrate and label each tool.

Name ____ Date ____________________

I See, I Saw

Write the letter of the correct answer next to each brief definition or description. You may use a dictionary.

______	1. has a long, narrow blade with fine teeth; used to produce ornamental work in thin wood or metal	a.	**hacksaw**
______	2. for cutting across the grain of wood	b.	**bucksaw**
______	3. power-driven saw with a narrow vertical blade used to cut sharp curves	c.	**fretsaw**
______	4. has tough, fine-toothed blade stretched tight in a frame; used for cutting metal	d.	**coping saw**
______	5. has narrow, short blade set in recessed handle; used for cutting designs in wood	e.	**backsaw**
______	6. electric saw consisting of a toothed disk rotating at high speed	f.	**band saw**
______	7. coarse-toothed saw for cutting along the grain of wood	g.	**crosscut saw**
______	8. power saw with toothed metal band coupled to the circumference of two wheels	h.	**ripsaw**
______	9. wood-cutting saw usually set in an H-shaped frame	i.	**circular saw**
______	10. saw reinforced by a metal band along its back edge	j.	**jigsaw**

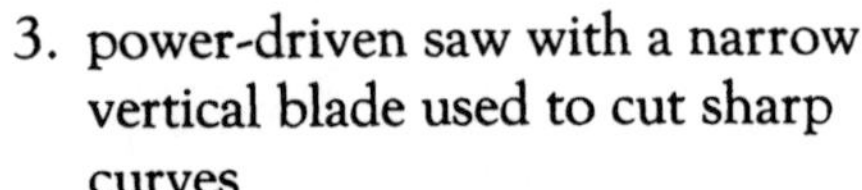

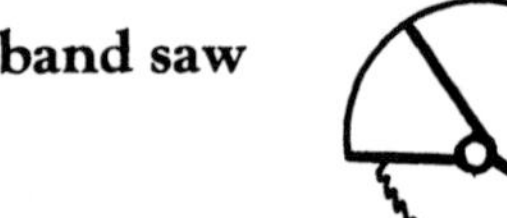

I Saw It in the Dictionary On the back of this sheet of paper, write a definition for each of the following words: **sawbones, sawbuck,. sawed-off, sawfly, sawhorse, sawmill, saw-toothed, sawyer.**

Name ______________________________ Date ______________

Computer Words

b i n a r y d e b u g i n t e r f a c e i n i t i a l i z e p i x e l

There are ten words in the letters at the top and bottom of this page. Separate the letters into words, then write the correct word on each line below. You may use a dictionary.

1. The ______________________ is a point at which independent systems interact.
2. The output of a computer in typewritten or printed form is called the ______________________.
3. A computer screen is called a ______________________.
4. A ______________________ is a single digit in a binary system.
5. The capacity of a computer for storing information is called ______________________.
6. A ______________________ is one million bytes of memory.
7. ______________________ refers to a numbering system with a base of two, using only the digits 0 and 1.
8. To ______________________ a computer program is to search for and eliminate malfunctioning elements or errors.
9. One of the many tiny picture elements that make up a computer screen graphic image is a ______________________.
10. To set a program to a starting position is to ______________________ it.

b i t m e g a b y t e p r i n t o u t m e m o r y m o n i t o r

What's the Difference? The computer and the robot are both machines designed by humans to help make our work easier. What are the differences between a computer and a robot? On a separate sheet of paper, write a two-paragraph explanation of the differences.

Name ______________________ Date ______________

The Sound of Weapons

Each word below names a tool used as a weapon. The word is spelled the way it sounds. After each phonetic spelling, write the actual spelling of the word. Then write the letter of the correct definition in front of each number. You may use a dictionary.

______ 1. **spir** _ _ _ _ _

______ 2. **hŏŏk** _ _ _ _

______ 3. **bō ləs** _ _ _ _ _

______ 4. **bō** _ _ _

______ 5. **sling** _ _ _ _ _

______ 6. **kuj əl** _ _ _ _ _ _

______ 7. **snar** _ _ _ _ _

______ 8. **bōō mə rang** _ _ _ _ _ _ _ _ _

______ 9. **net** _ _ _

______ 10. **har pōōn** _ _ _ _ _ _ _

______ 11. **blō gun** _ _ _ _ _ _ _

______ 12. **ăr ō** _ _ _ _ _

a. curved, flexible strip of material strung taut from one end to other; used to launch arrows
b. a long shaft with a sharply pointed head
c. a long, narrow pipe through which darts or pellets are blown
d. a short, heavy club, suitable as a weapon
e. an openwork fabric made of threads or cords that are knotted together at regular intervals
f. curved or sharply bent piece of material used to catch, drag, or suspend something
g. a looped strap in which a stone is whirled and then let fly
h. a long shaft with a barbed head
i. rope with weights attached; used to catch animals by entangling their legs
j. a flat, curved wooden weapon that can be hurled so it returns to the thrower
k. a straight, thin shaft shot from a bow
l. a trapping device consisting of a noose used for capturing birds and other small animals

Chronological Order On a separate sheet of paper, make a list of at least twenty different weapons. Then organize the list into chronological order, beginning with the oldest weapon and ending with the most recent.

Name ______________________________ Date ______________

Name the Tool

Adz, awl, ax, chisel, file, grapple, level, parbuckle, pick, pliers, tongs, windlass – these are all particular tools. Write the correct term under each illustration below. You may use a dictionary.

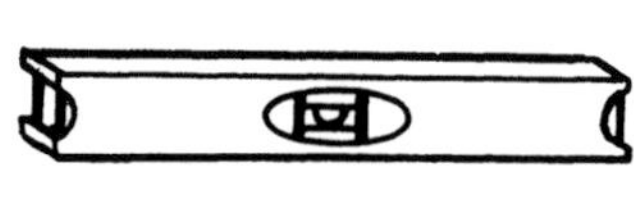

1. ______________ 2. ______________ 3. ______________

4. ______________ 5. ______________ 6. ______________

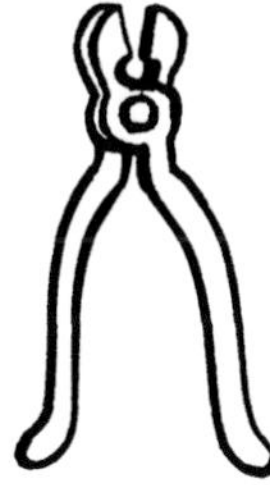

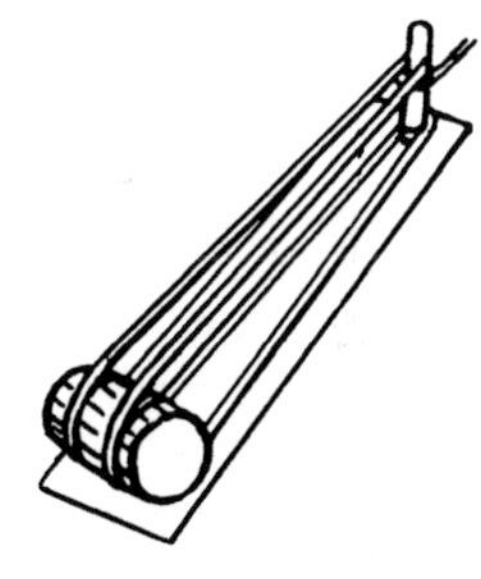

7. ______________ 8. ______________ 9. ______________

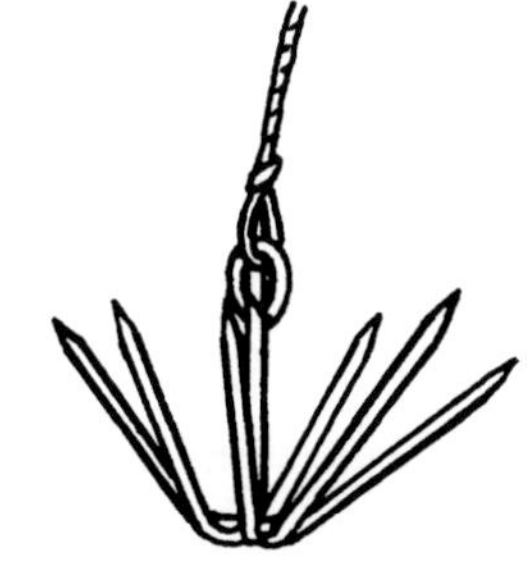

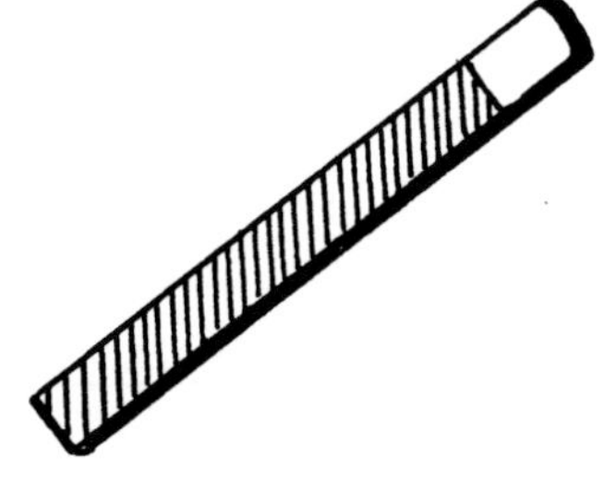

10. ______________ 11. ______________ 12. ______________

Invent a Tool Every day somebody takes out a patent on a particular type of invention. Many of these inventions are tools. Think about something that could be done better with a tool that doesn't yet exist. "Invent" the tool. On the back of this sheet of paper, describe the tool. Give its name, and explain what it does and how it works.

Name ______________________________ Date ______________

Agricultural Tools and Machines

Write an answer to each question below. You may use the dictionary.

1. How do a **sickle** and a **machete** differ? ______________________________

____

____

2. How are a **flail** and a **combine** different? ______________________________

____

____

3. What does a **plow** do to the land, and what does a **harrow** do? ______________

____

____

4. How are a **hoe** and a **cultivator** similar? ______________________________

____

____

5. For what is a **windrower** used? ______________________________

____

____

6. What are **shears**? ______________________________

____

____

7. What is a grain **drill**? ______________________________

____

____

Advertising Slogans The advertising slogan for John Deere tractors is "Nothing runs like a Deere." Choose two of the agricultural tools above. Then, on a separate sheet of paper, invent a brand name and an appropriate slogan for each.

Name ______________________________ Date ______________

Tool Crossword

Solve the crossword puzzle by writing the correct word in each blank. You may use a dictionary.

Across

1. flat-bladed hand tool for leveling or spreading mortar
3. bristles bound together and attached to a handle; used for sweeping
5. machine on which wood is spun and shaped by a cutting tool
6. cutting tool with a sharp blade and a handle
7. device used to secure a door, operated by a key
8. machine for transferring a liquid from one container to another through pipes or tubes
9. piece of tapered wood or metal inserted into a crevice and used to split, tighten, or secure
10. carpenter's tool with adjustable blade for smoothing and leveling wood
12. cylindrical rod incised with one or more helical spiral threads
16. short-handled hammer with a cylindrical head of wood; used to drive a chisel or wedge
18. small, short-handled ax
20. mill or other machine that runs on energy generated by a wheel of blades rotated by the wind
21. chisel with a rounded, troughlike blade used to scoop or dig wood
23. machine for hoisting and moving heavy objects by means of cables attached to a movable boom
24. long pole extending upward at an angle from the mast of a derrick to support or guide objects that are lifted or suspended

Down

1. hand-held implement used to accomplish work
2. solid disk or circular ring that turns around an axle
4. an inclined passageway connecting different levels
5. simple machine consisting of a rigid bar that pivots on a fixed fulcrum
9. hand tool with jaw for gripping, turning, or twisting an object such as a nut, bolt, or pipe
11. slim, pointed piece of metal hammered into something as a fastener
12. a T-shaped or L-shaped instrument for drawing or testing right angles
13. clamping device consisting of two jaws closed or opened by a lever
14. small, slender pointed tool with eye at one end through which thread is passed
15. small block of metal or wood with a central, threaded hole, designed to fit around a bolt or screw
17. threaded rod used as a fastener, secured by a nut that is tightened around it
19. tool for boring holes in wood
22. plain or notched piece of wood or metal designed to hold parts of a structure in place, usually adjusted by a screw or key

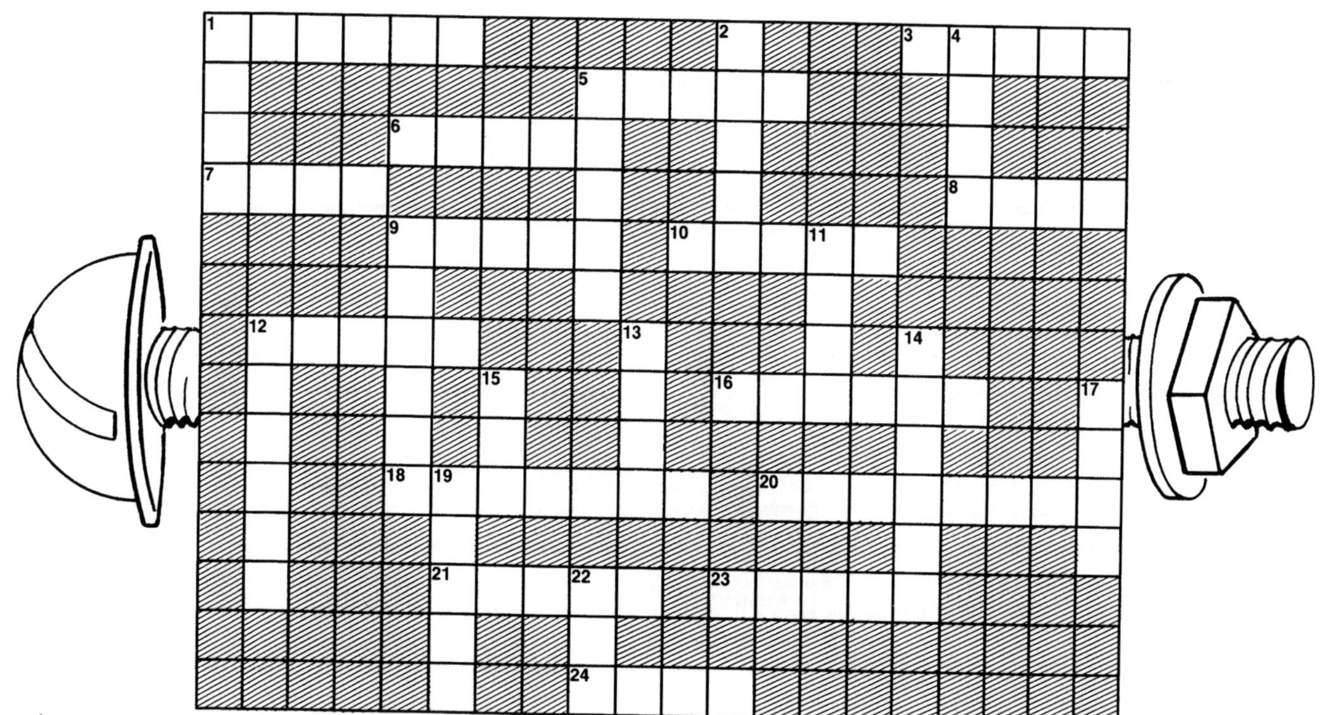

Tool Classification On a separate sheet of paper, label three columns: Basement, Kitchen, Outdoors. List as many tools as you can think of in each category (depending on area of use). Try to list at least thirty tools in each category.

Name ____________________ Date ____________

Picture Perfect

Pictured below are nine common kitchen tools. Identify each tool by writing its name beneath the correct picture. Then write a definition of each tool. You may use a dictionary.

1. ____________________

6. ____________________

2. ____________________

7. ____________________

3. ____________________

8. ____________________

4. ____________________

9. ____________________

5. ____________________

10. ____________________

Tool Rhyme On the back of this sheet of paper, write a list of ten words that rhyme with ***tool***. Then write a poem about tools using at least five of the rhyming words.

Name ______________________________ Date ______________

More Computer Words

Read each definition below. Circle the one word that is the correct term for each definition. You may use a dictionary.

1. instrument that changes signals from one form to another	**joystick**	**modem**	**terminal**
2. computer that uses numbers to perform logical and numerical calculations	**digital**	**pixel**	**analog**
3. round, flat plate coated with magnetic substance on which data can be stored	**printout**	**disk**	**text**
4. the part of a computer system that operates on data	**processor**	**monitor**	**network**
5. an integrated circuit; a tiny complex of electronic components	**pixel**	**scroll**	**chip**
6. computer that uses voltages instead of numbers	**mainframe**	**floppy**	**analog**
7. the coded instructions and data that direct a digital computer to solve a problem	**modem**	**program**	**disk**
8. a string of binary digits operated on as a basic unit	**bit**	**byte**	**glitch**
9. a device connected to a computer to provide auxiliary functions	**peripheral**	**terminal**	**monitor**
10. a malfunction or failure to function properly; error	**glitch**	**scroll**	**crunch**
11. the program associated with a computer system stored on disk	**peripheral**	**software**	**hardware**
12. one billionth of a second	**picosecond**	**gigabit**	**nanosecond**

Computer Outline On the back of this sheet of paper, write an outline for a speech on computers. Discuss their history, current uses, and possible future uses. Outline on two levels (Roman numerals and capital letters).

Name ______________________________ Date ______________

The National Pastime

Study the diagram below. Write the correct vocabulary term on each line of the diagram. You may use the dictionary.

fence	left field	batter's box	pitcher's mound
dugout	right field	catcher's box	warning track
baseline	center field	coach's box	on-deck circle

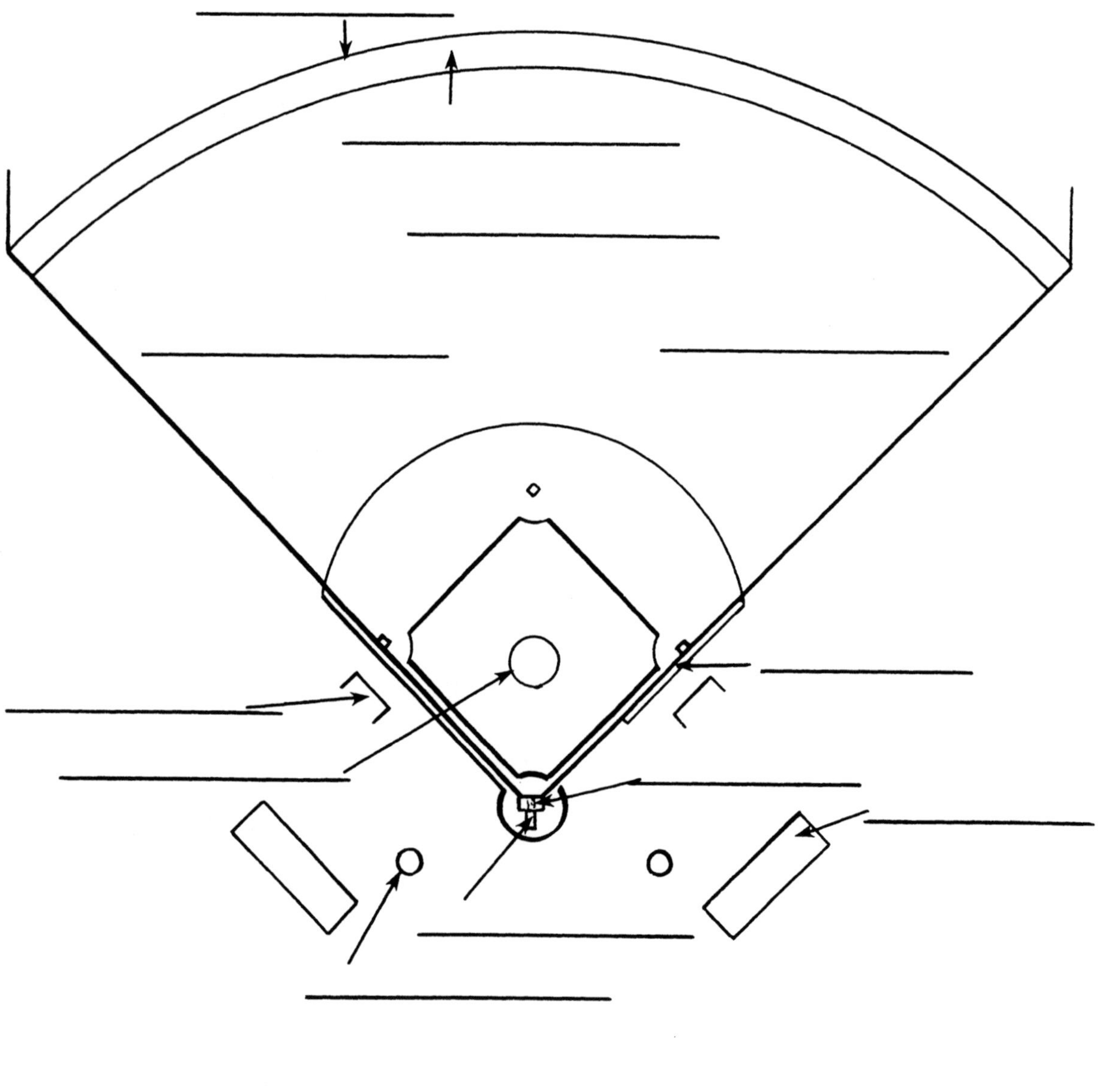

Baseball Teams On a separate sheet of paper, label one column National League and the other column American League. List as many of the twenty-six major-league baseball teams as you can, putting each in its proper league.

Name ______________________________ Date ______________

Which Sport?

Write the letter of the correct answer next to each brief definition. Then turn this sheet of paper over and write twelve sentences, using one of the twelve sports words in each. You may use a dictionary.

______	1. sport of shooting arrows with a bow	a. **cycling**
______	2. sport of riding in gondolas attached to airtight bags filled with hot air	b. **sailing**
______	3. sport of riding or racing two-wheeled, tubular metal-framed vehicles	c. **golf**
______	4. dueling with swords	d. **billiards**
______	5. throwing a disk to somebody who tries to catch it	e. **Frisbee**
______	6. slow running	f. **figure skating**
______	7. sport of riding a heavier-than-air launch through the air	g. **ballooning**
______	8. played on links with ball and clubs	h. **karting**
______	9. sport of riding or racing motorless, oarless boats	i. **jogging**
______	10. gliding over the ice in precision patterns	j. **archery**
______	11. played on pool table with balls and cue stick	k. **fencing**
______	12. racing of small, light-weight, no-frills race cars	l. **hang gliding**
______	13. sport of jumping from a plane and executing free-fall maneuvers before opening a parachute	m. **surfing**
______	14. traveling over the snow on long, thin strips of wood fastened to shoes	n. **skiing**
______	15. sport of riding in toward the shore on the crest of a wave	o. **sky diving**

Future Drama On a separate sheet of paper, write a scene from a movie about thirtieth-century archaeologists who have found a Frisbee and are trying to determine what it was.

Name ______________________________ Date ______________

Basketball Rhymes

Read each basketball definition below. Write the answer on the line. The answer rhymes with the boldfaced word or words. (Remember that words that rhyme are not always spelled similarly.) You may use the dictionary.

1. to bounce the ball off the floor

   Don't **quibble** about that ______________ .

2. to run into a defensive player who has established position

   Lance likes to **barge** and ______________ when he plays.

3. goal made by leaping and pushing the ball down into the basket

   The clock went **clunk** as Claudia made the ______________ .

4. the goal

   Kyle's final ______________ put the opponents in the **casket**.

5. an infraction of the rules that prohibit illegal physical contact

   "A wise **owl** does not ______________ ," lectured the coach.

6. to bounce the ball off the backboard toward the basket

   Hank can ______________ a shot with the best of them.

7. one-handed overhead shot made with the back arm when the body is turned sideways to the basket

   They **shook** when Kathi sank her ______________ .

8. a determined advance with the ball

   "Don't give me that **jive**, give me a ______________ !" shouted the coach.

9. to pass to a teammate near the basket

   Reid will ______________ the ball to **Sneed**.

10. the rectangular playing area

    The ______________ was Wayne's personal **fort**.

11. the free throw area

    Pass to **me** when I'm in the ______________ .

12. either of two players who usually bring the ball out of the backcourt and start plays

    The ______________ sat in the **yard**.

Sports Classification On a separate sheet of paper, label three columns: Handball Games, Football Games, and Ball-and-Stick Games. Classify as many sports as you can into these three categories. Try to name at least five sports in each category.

Name ______________________________ Date ______________

New Sports Words

Each year thousands of new words are accepted into the language. The words below are newly accepted words. Fill in the blanks by writing the correct word on each line. You may use the dictionary.

jock	**rabbit**	**biathlon**	**orienteering**
dojo	**rollout**	**turnover**	**schussboomer**
stuff	**platoon**	**sailboard**	**isometrics**

1. A track-team runner who sets a fast pace for the first part of the race, a ____________________ usually does so to help a teammate.
2. To ____________________ is to use alternate players at the same position.
3. A type of exercise, ____________________ involves the tensing or using of one set of muscles against another set or against an immovable object.
4. A room in which akido, karate, or other self-defense martial arts are taught is a ____________________ .
5. A play in which the quarterback moves laterally in preparing to throw a pass is a ____________________ .
6. A ____________________ is a small, flat sailboat designed for one or two passengers.
7. A skier who skis downhill expertly at high speeds is a ____________________ .
8. To ____________________ is to throw or drive a ball or puck into a goal from very close range.
9. The loss of possession of the ball because of an error by the offensive team is a ____________________ .
10. A timed competition in which runners run across country, ____________________ requires that the participants follow a map and use a compass.
11. A high school or college athlete is a ____________________ .
12. A ____________________ is an athletic contest of cross-country skiing and rifle sharpshooting.

Professional Sports On the back of this sheet of paper, write two paragraphs discussing the positive and negative aspects of professional sports.

Name ______________________________ Date ______________

Bowling Picture

Study the diagram below. Write the correct vocabulary word on each line of the diagram. You may use a dictionary.

pit	**spots**	**approach**	**kingpin**	**thumb hole**
span	**gutter**	**headpin**	**finger hole**	**foul line**

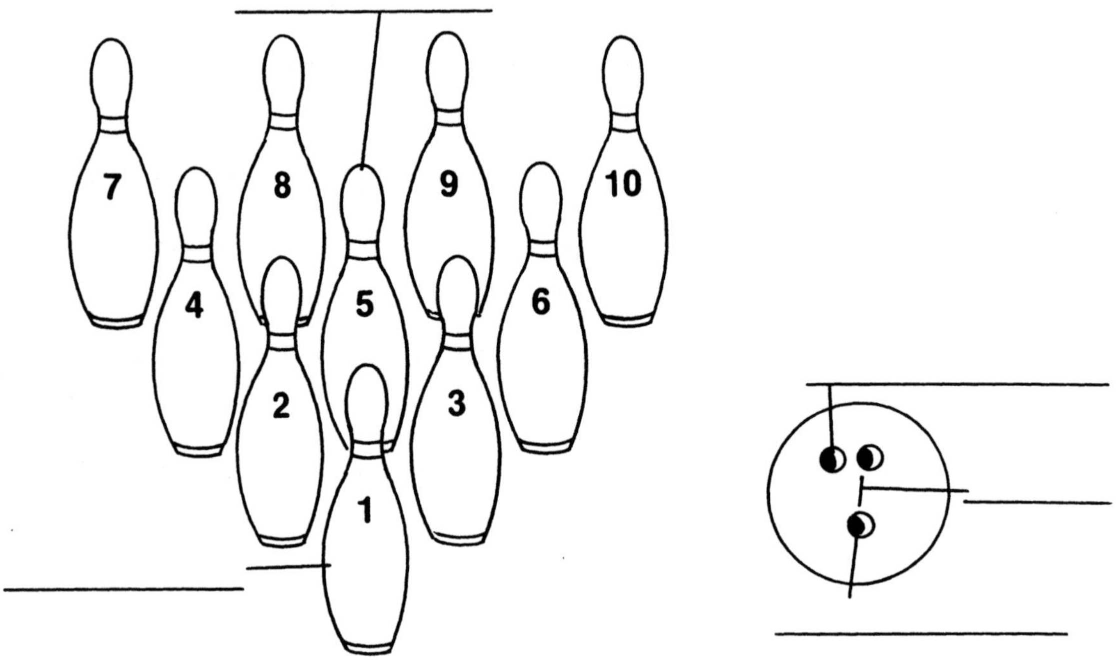

7 8 9 10

4 5 6

2 3

1

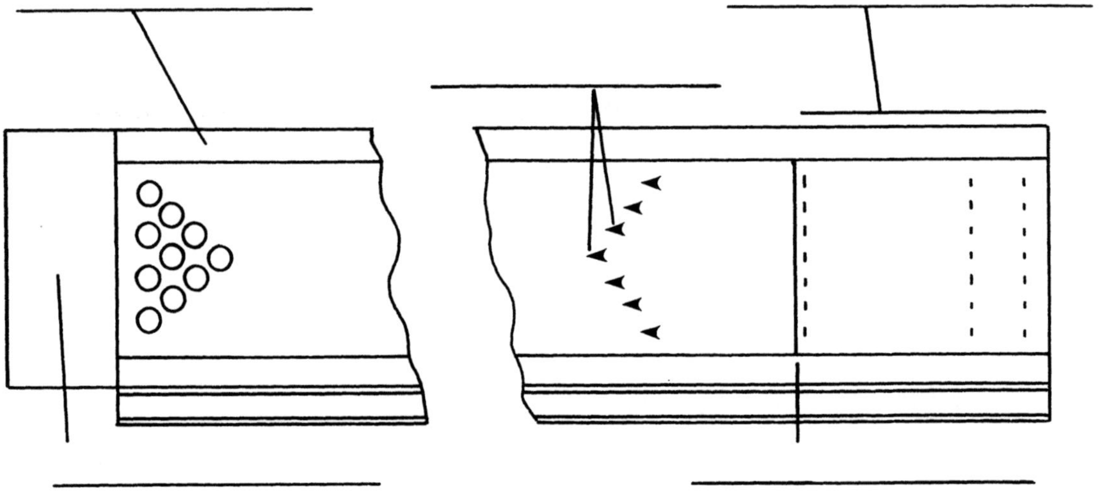

Scoring Read about how to keep score in bowling. Prepare a speech for class, explaining how to keep score in bowling. Be certain to prepare visual aids (such as a bowling score sheet) to use with your talk.

Name ______________________________ Date ______________

Sports Picture

Look at each sports term below. Under the Picture column, write the letter of the picture that goes with the term. Under the Definition column, write the letter of the matching definition. You may use a dictionary.

Picture	Term	Definition
______	1. **puck**	______
______	2. **hurdle**	______
______	3. **lacrosse racket**	______
______	4. **javelin**	______
______	5. **horse**	______
______	6. **squash racket**	______
______	7. **water ski**	______
______	8. **shuttlecock**	______
______	9. **cue**	______
______	10. **hammer**	______
______	11. **downhill ski**	______
______	12. **crampon**	______

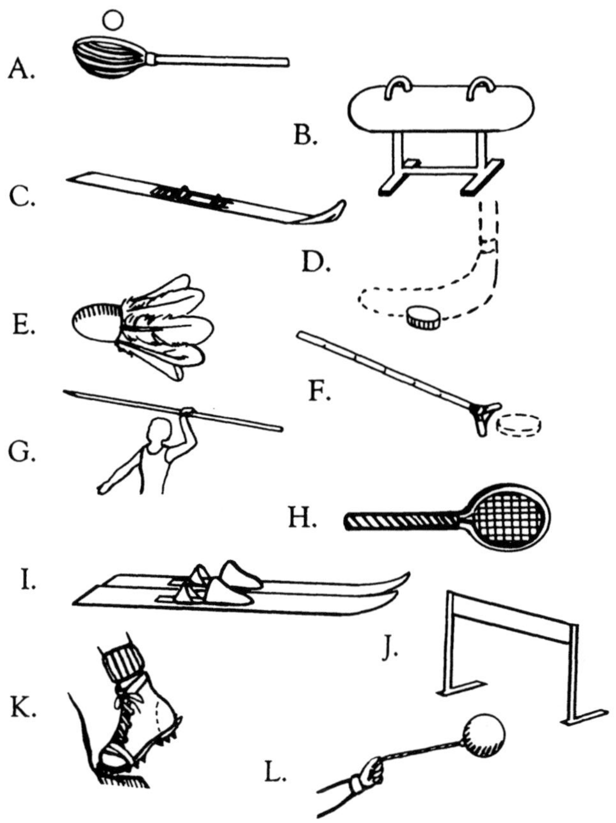

A.
B.
C.
D.
E.
F.
G.
H.
I.
J.
K.
L.

O. a sixteen-pound metal ball hung from a wire handle and thrown for distance in track-and-field events
P. either of a pair of iron plates fastened to shoes to prevent slipping in ice climbing
Q. a light spear for throwing in track and field events
R. one of a pair of wide runners of wood with bindings for the feet, used to tow a person across the surface of the water
S. a vulcanized rubber disk which each ice hockey team tries to drive into the goal
T. a long shovel-like stick used to push the disks in shuffleboard
U. a very long-handled light bat with a network of catgut in an oval frame, used for hitting a soft rubber ball against a wall in an enclosed court
V. a long-handled pouched racket used to advance a small rubber ball across a field into the goal
W. a series of framelike barriers over which runners must leap in a special race
X. one of a pair of long, thin runners of wood fastened to shoes and used for gliding over snow
Y. a rounded piece of cork with a flat end from which feathers project, used in badminton
Z. a padded block on legs, used for jumping or vaulting in gymnastics

Sports Speech Prepare a five-minute speech on good sportsmanship versus bad sportsmanship. Give definitions of each term and examples of each term from current sporting events.

Name ______________________________ Date ______________

Twenty Sports

The names of twenty sports are hidden below. The words run from left to right or from top to bottom. Circle each of the twenty words. You may use a dictionary.

A B C D E J I H G F K L M N O A S R Q P T
U V W R A C Q U E T B A L L X S Y Z E R P
S K A T I N G O X A O J E D I U N D S W O
R E V R M H C B G L Q U Z Y T R P I K F L
A C B P A R A C H U T I N G C F D V E F O
G R H I G O N M L K P Q R S A I T I U V W
X O S Y Z E R O Y S T P K F A N B N G L V
Q Q Q U Z E V R M O H C D I N G S G W R O
O U U X A S O E J F E N C I N G E D C B L
A E A J I K H G F T O N M L K A S R Q P L
X T S W V I U T O B R E Z Y E K V R M H E
C B H G L I Q U B A S K E T B A L L Z R Y
W S N I D N E J O L O A X O Y Y T P K F B
A B C D E G F G H L C I J K L A M N O P A
Q R S A T U V W X Y C Z H O C K E Y E R L
B R E Z Y T U V W X E A S R Q I P K L M L
H S W I M M I N G O R J I K H N G F A B C
D E J I H F G H L M N O S E D G C B A F K
P Q R S A O N M K T E N N I S L K P T U V
H I K I N G W W E I G H T L I F T I N G R

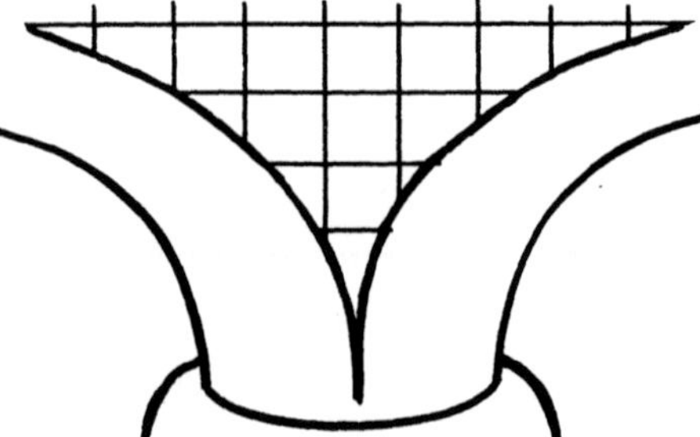

Defining Terms On the back of this sheet of paper, define any ten of the twenty hidden sports words.

Name ______________________________ Date ______________

Football Compounds

Each football word on this page is a compound word—one word made out of two separate words (such as *gold* + *fish* = *goldfish*). Correctly combine one word from the top goal with one word from the bottom goal. Write each word on the correct line. You may use a dictionary.

kick	**half**	**hand**	**grid**	**wish**	**off**
pig	**touch**	**back**	**quarter**	**goal**	**over**

______________ 1. a football field

______________ 2. offensive back who receives the snap

______________ 3. a free kick to put the ball in play

______________ 4. six-point score made by advancing ball beyond the opposing team's goal line

______________ 5. offensive backfield player who functions as receiver or ball carrier

______________ 6. either of two uprights that mark the sides of the goal

______________ 7. a football

______________ 8. the offensive and defensive backs

______________ 9. over the line of scrimmage or ahead of the ball before play has begun

______________ 10. act of handing the ball to a teammate

______________ 11. a variation of the T-formation that utilizes an unbalanced line and in which the halfbacks are to the side of and physically behind the fullback

______________ 12. an extra 15-minute period of play to decide a tied game

skin	**time**	**field**	**down**	**iron**	**back**
back	**off**	**post**	**side**	**off**	**bone**

Football Experience On a separate sheet of paper, write a description of what it feels like to be a spectator at a January football playoff in an outdoor stadium in which the temperature is minus 20 degrees Fahrenheit.

Name ______________________ Date ______________

More Sports

Read each brief sports definition or description. Circle the one word from the three boldfaced words that best matches the definition. You may use a dictionary.

1. team of ten or twelve, uses rackets and ball on field	**lacrosse**	**rugby**	**jai-alai**
2. sliding a heavy disk of stone on ice at a target	**boules**	**squash**	**curling**
3. British game of ninepins	**skittles**	**jai-alai**	**cricket**
4. old game much like field hockey	**curling**	**bandy**	**rounders**
5. like handball, popular in Latin America	**hurling**	**boules**	**jai-alai**
6. team of fifteen, continuous action, oval ball	**bandy**	**rugby**	**lacrosse**
7. game like handball and tennis	**squash**	**cricket**	**sumo**
8. British form of baseball	**rounders**	**croquet**	**snooker**
9. sport of exploring caves	**spelunking**	**roque**	**hurling**
10. variety of the game of pool	**snooker**	**roque**	**boules**
11. team of eleven, uses ball, bats, and wickets	**croquet**	**kendo**	**cricket**
12. long, heavy pole "tossed" in Gaelic games to test muscular strength	**javelin**	**caber**	**kendo**

A–Z Sports On the back of this sheet of paper, write the letters A through Z in a column. Can you think of a sport for each letter of the alphabet? List as many sports as you can; how close to twenty-six can you get?

Name ______________________________ Date ______________

Baseball Crossword

Solve the crossword puzzle by writing the correct word in each blank. You may use a dictionary.

Across

4. screen behind home plate
6. line extending from home plate to first or third base and beyond
8. a fair ball that clears the fence
10. the tally of balls and strikes
12. raised area where the pitcher stands
13. offensive player on base
14. an inexperienced, first-year player
15. eccentric player or eccentric person
17. a _____ hitter is one sent in to take another player's turn at bat
18. a ball that is not fair
21. defensive player who throws the ball to the batter
22. the playing field beyond the infield
24. to break for and run to a base safely
25. a game in which the opponent is prevented from scoring

Down

1. one is at each corner of the infield
2. the official responsible for the conduct of the game
3. an illegal motion by the pitcher
5. the defensive player behind home plate
6. a pitched ball that misses the strike zone
7. a pitched ball at which the batter swings and misses
9. situation in which a base runner is trapped off base between two fielders, one of whom has the ball
10. a pitch that breaks downward and to the side
11. two consecutive games on the same day
15. to lose a game due to an inability or refusal to play because of a rule infraction
16. batted ball that soars high into the air
19. infield defensive player who covers the area between second and third base
20. a metal projection on the sole of a baseball shoe
23. a two-base hit

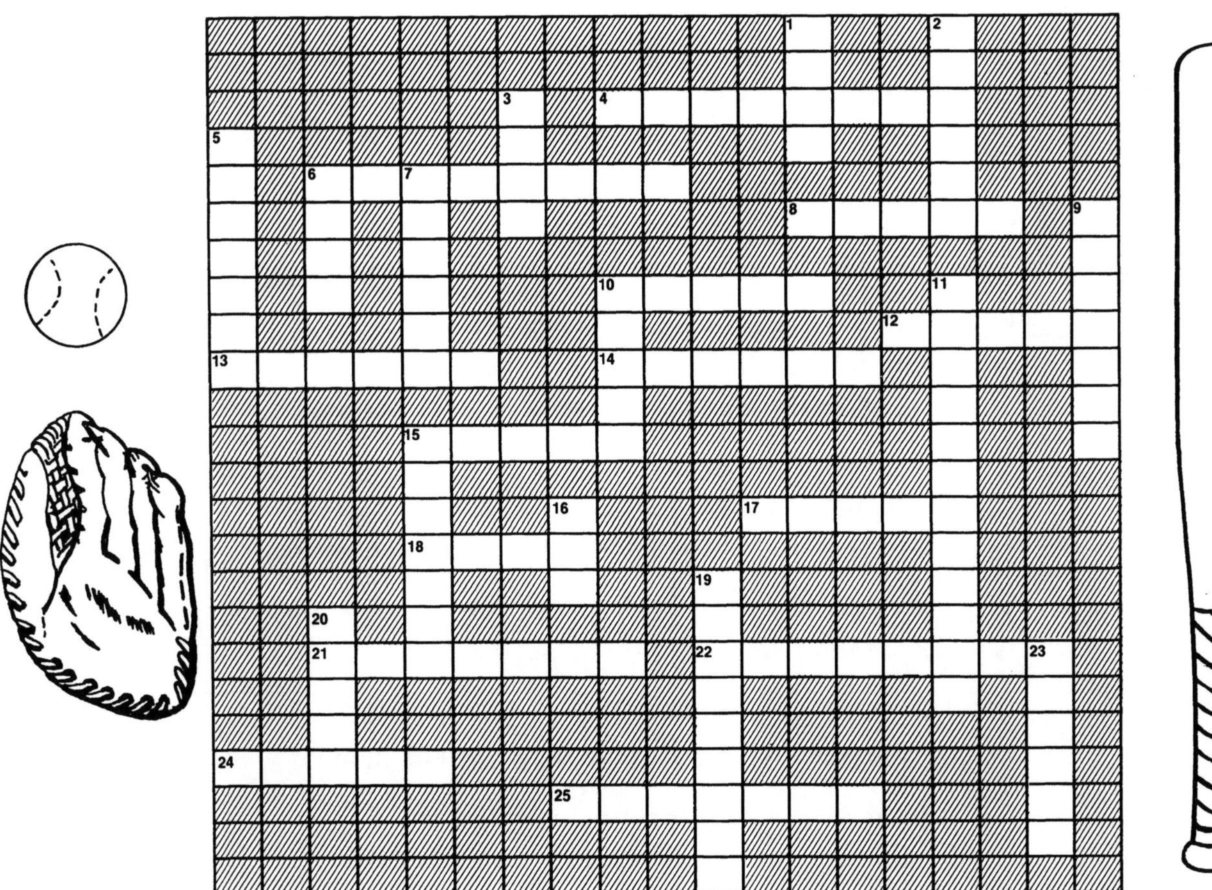

The Mudville Nine Read the poem "Casey at the Bat" by Ernest Lawrence Thayer. On a separate sheet of paper, write an analysis of the poem.

Name ______________________________ Date ______________

Words About Literature

Read each definition below. Write the letter of the answer on each line. You may use a dictionary.

______ 1. A statement that seems to contradict itself, but which contains a basis of truth is a
(a) **parable** (b) **hyperbole** (c) **paradox**

______ 2. A recurring element within a single work is called a
(a) **flashback** (b) **motif** (c) **theme**

______ 3. A device by which a writer expresses a meaning opposite the stated or obvious meaning is
(a) **drama** (b) **allegory** (c) **irony**

______ 4. A literary type or class is called a
(a) **philippic** (b) **paradigm** (c) **genre**

______ 5. A figure of speech in which emphasis is achieved by extreme exaggeration is
(a) **hyperbole** (b) **proverb** (c) **denouement**

______ 6. A literary work produced for the sole purpose of providing the writer with money is a
(a) **lampoon** (b) **potboiler** (c) **chronicle**

______ 7. An expressed comparison between two unlike things usually using the words *like* or *as* is a
(a) **simile** (b) **metaphor** (c) **personification**

______ 8. The scornful or witty ridiculing of a subject in order to discredit vice or folly is called
(a) **verisimilitude** (b) **satire** (c) **bathos**

______ 9. The unknotting of events following the major climax of a plot is called the
(a) **panegyric** (b) **paradigm** (c) **denouement**

______ 10. The central idea or thesis of a poem, novel, or play is its
(a) **point of view** (b) **theme** (c) **saga**

______ 11. The most important character in a play or story is the
(a) **protagonist** (b) **paradigm** (c) **paradox**

______ 12. A reference to a familiar person or thing is an
(a) **illusion** (b) **allegory** (c) **allusion**

I Am a Book In a dictionary or literary dictionary, look up the word ***personification***. On a separate sheet of paper, write a story in which you personify a book.

Name ______________________________ Date ______________

The Mystery of It All

Read the scene below. Fill in each blank with the correct vocabulary word. You may use the dictionary.

ink	**paper**	**writing**	**manuscript**	**cacography**
quill	**cipher**	**alphabet**	**inscription**	**calligraphy**

Halves: Watnot! This ______________ (written composition) is written in ______________ (a method of transforming a text in order to conceal its meaning).

Watnot: I say, Halves! What extraordinary ______________ (bad handwriting)!

Halves: I disagree, Watnot. I would say that the person who wrote this has ______________ (beautiful handwriting), which she has sought to disguise.

Watnot: *She?* Surely, Halves, that is going a bit too far. Look at the ______________ (felted sheet of vegetable fibers laid down on a fine screen from a water suspension). It's coarse, cheap, and. . .*(SNIFF)* smells of tobacco!

Halves: All part of the game, Watnot. Look at the ______________ (colored liquid material for writing). It's lavender! And this code was written with a(n) ______________ (pen made from the hollow barrel of a feather). Only someone with beautiful handwriting would attempt to write with a quill.

Watnot: Yes, but I say, Halves—how are we going to get at the meaning of it all? Why, why. . .it isn't even written with a(n) ______________ (set of letters or characters with which a language is written).

Halves: You're mistaken, my dear Watnot. I'm beginning to get the picture already. The first words appear to be a(n) ______________ (written dedication of a book or work of art). It says, "To all code breakers everywhere: Long live ______________ (the act of forming characters on a surface with an instrument)!

Watnot: I say, Halves. Rather silly, don't you think?

Halves: Not at all, Watnot. Where would you be if you couldn't scribble those stories about me?

Graphology Write a definition of ***graphology*** on the back of this sheet of paper. Exchange papers with another student. Write a one-paragraph analysis of the other student's character based on his or her handwriting.

Name ______________________________ Date ______________

Give Me Music, Music, Music

c a l y p s o j a z z z y d e c o r o c k a n d r o l l f o l k m u s i c r a g t i m e b l u e s s w i n g

There are fifteen words or phrases in the letters at the top and bottom of this page. Separate the letters into words. Then write the correct word on each line below. You may use a dictionary.

1. ______________ originated in New Orleans as improvised music; it often features saxophone, clarinet, and/or trumpet.
2. ______________ has a strong, regular rhythm and evolved in the 1950s from both jazz and blues.
3. ______________ combines rock-and-roll and country music.
4. Folk-singing evangelism is called ______________ .
5. A dance music, ______________ has elements of soul with a Latin American beat.
6. ______________ is a kind of Southern string-band music with high-pitched harmony.
7. ______________ contains highly embellished melodies and fugal forms.
8. Originating in Jamaica, ______________ was influenced by rock and roll and calypso.
9. From southern Louisiana, ______________ features the guitar, washboard, and accordion.
10. ______________ is black folk music with a slow tempo and melancholy words.
11. Symphonies, sonatas, and concertos are examples of ______________ music.
12. ______________ is jazz music with a steady, lively rhythm, usually played by a large dance band.
13. An American folk music of 1890–1915, ______________ has strong syncopation and fast, even time.
14. ______________ is music made and handed down among the common people.
15. From Trinidad, ______________ originally featured satirical ballads with a wrenched syllabic stress on words.

c l a s s i c a l r o c k a b i l l y g o s p e l r e g g a e b a r o q u e d i s c o b l u e g r a s s

What Is Music? On a separate sheet of paper, write two paragraphs on music. The first paragraph should discuss music from a purely technical, dictionary-definition point of view. The second paragraph should discuss music from a personal, emotional point of view.

Name ______________________________ Date ______________

Split Screen

Each vocabulary word has been broken into two parts. The first part is in the left-hand TV screen; the second part is in the right-hand TV screen. Put the word parts together correctly. Then write the correct word next to each brief definition or description. You may use a dictionary.

anchor **docu**
sani **pro**
spin- **viewer**
non **mini**
voice **net**

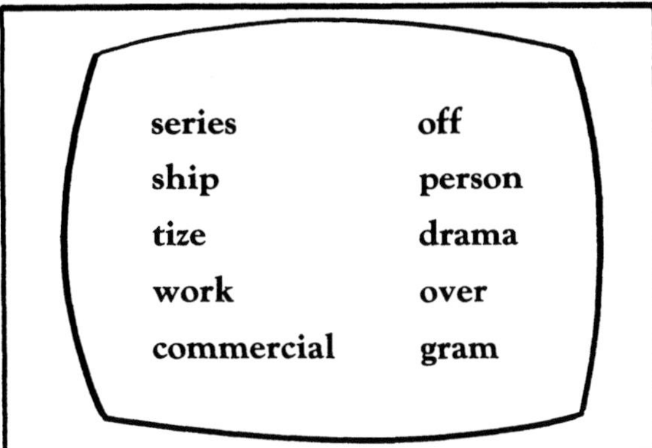

__________ 1. a scheduled television show

__________ 2. a group of TV broadcasting stations that produces programs for broadcast by stations within the group

__________ 3. the narrator or coordinator of a TV newscast in which several reporters take part

__________ 4. television that is not sponsored or supported by advertisers

__________ 5. a TV screenplay presentation of events based on fact

__________ 6. several episodes in sequence that make up a TV dramatic presentation

__________ 7. a TV show starring a character who had a popular supporting role in another series

__________ 8. the people who make up a particular TV audience

__________ 9. to make something more acceptable (as television often does) by removing its unpleasant or offensive features

__________ 10. the voice of a narrator who does not appear as a character on camera

Television Sentences On a separate sheet of paper, write ten sentences. Each sentence should use one of the ten vocabulary words above; each sentence should try to give a specific, actual example from television programs or commercials.

Name ______________________________ Date ______________

Poetry or Prose?

You will need a dictionary in order to complete the activity below. First, define ***poetry*** and ***prose*** in the space provided. Then write each of the twenty words under the proper category, Poetry or Prose. The twenty words are: **antinovel, autobiography, ballad, bildungsroman, biography, canto, couplet, doggerel, elegy, epistle, essay, fable, haiku, limerick, novel, novella, ode, roman à clef, sonnet, stanza.**

Poetry is ______________________________

____

____

____

Prose is ______________________________

____

____

____

	Poetry	**Prose**
1.	____________	____________
2.	____________	____________
3.	____________	____________
4.	____________	____________
5.	____________	____________
6.	____________	____________
7.	____________	____________
8.	____________	____________
9.	____________	____________
10.	____________	____________

The Play's the Thing On a separate sheet of paper, define each of these words: **antagonist, burlesque, catharsis, climax, deuteragonist, hubris, masque, melodrama, protagonist, soliloquy.**

Name ______________________________ Date ______________

Fit to Print

Column, deadline, editorial, feature, paparazzo, parajournalism, publish, samizdat, stringer, syndicated. Write each word in the correct space. You may use a dictionary.

1. ☐☐☐☐■☐☐☐☐☐☐☐☐☐
2. ☐☐☐☐■☐☐☐☐
3. ☐☐☐■☐☐
4. ☐☐☐☐■☐☐☐☐
5. ☐☐☐☐■☐☐☐☐
6. ☐☐■☐☐☐☐
7. ☐☐☐☐■☐☐☐
8. ☐☐☐☐■☐☐☐☐☐
9. ☐☐☐☐☐■☐
10. ☐☐■☐☐☐☐☐

1. journalism that is not objective, that is heavily colored by the opinions of the reporter
2. a newspaper article that gives the opinions of the editors or publishers
3. one in a regular series of newspaper articles
4. a freelance photographer who aggressively pursues celebrities for the purpose of taking cadid photos of them
5. a news correspondent who works for a paper or magazine on a part-time basis
6. a story or article or department in a paper or magazine that is given special prominence
7. the time after which copy is not accepted for a particular issue of a publication
8. sold to a business that sells materials for publication in a number of newspapers or periodicals at the same time
9. to produce in print and release to the public
10. self-published literature in the USSR, clandestinely circulated because it is or would be suppressed by the government

Define Your Terms What is the word spelled out in the boldfaced blocks above? On a separate sheet of paper, write several paragraphs in which you define the term and discuss its positive and negative contributions to our world.

Name ______________________________ Date ______________

The Not-So-Silent Screen

Each word below is spelled the way it sounds. After each phonetic spelling, write the actual spelling of the word. Then write the letter of the correct definition in front of each number. You may use a dictionary.

______ 1. **dä l ē** _ _ _ _ _

______ 2. **prə dōōs ər** _ _ _ _ _ _ _ _

______ 3. **gaf ər** _ _ _ _ _ _

______ 4. **sēn** _ _ _ _ _

______ 5. **frēz-frām** _ _ _ _ _ _-_ _ _ _ _

______ 6. **di rek tə r** _ _ _ _ _ _ _ _

______ 7. **siŋ krə nīz** _ _ _ _ _ _ _ _ _ _ _

______ 8. **rush** _ _ _ _

______ 9. **däk yə men tə rē** _ _ _ _ _ _ _ _ _ _ _

______ 10. **skrēn** _ _ _ _ _ _

a. person in charge of the financing and coordination of all activities for the creation of a motion picture

b. a part of a motion picture that makes up a unit of development

c. a white, flat surface upon which motion pictures are projected

d. person who plans the action and effects and supervises and instructs the actors and technicians in a motion picture

e. a low, wheeled platform on which a camera is mounted for moving it around the movie or television set

f. a movie or television program that shows or analyzes events or social conditions with no fictionalization

g. to adjust the picture and sound effects so they coincide perfectly

h. the head electrician on a movie or television set

i. a first print made after the filming of a scene; also called a daily

j. a single frame of a motion picture repeated so as to stop motion and give the effect of a still photograph for dramatic emphasis

Silent Screen On a separate sheet of paper, write three paragraphs discussing the acting in silent movies. How was it different from acting today? Why was it different? How did the introduction of sound change acting?

Name ______________________________ Date ______________

Heavy Words

Fill in the blanks below by writing the correct word on each line. You may use your dictionary.

cant	**vowel**	**consonant**	**hieroglyphic**
glyph	**harangue**	**semantics**	**mellifluous**
trite	**polyglot**	**cuneiform**	**gobbledygook**

1. ______________ writing is composed of pictorial characters.
2. To speak or write several languages is to be ______________ .
3. Wordy jargon, ______________ usually cannot be understood.
4. A symbol that conveys information in a nonverbal way is called a ______________ .
5. A ______________ is a speech sound made by a partial or complete obstruction of the air stream.
6. A bombastic, ranting speech is a ______________ .
7. ______________ is insincere use of pious words.
8. Writing that is composed of wedge-shaped characters is classified as ______________ .
9. ______________ is the study of word and phrase meanings.
10. Neither fresh nor original, a ______________ expression is one that has been overused and is thus boring.
11. A ______________ is a speech sound made without blocking the air stream and without audible friction.
12. A voice that has a smooth, rich flow is ______________ .

Phonetic Challenge Educators and others have made several attempts to write English phonetically. Read about some of these systems in the library. Then, using one of the phonetic alphabets, write out the sentences in this paragraph. Ask a friend to read the paragraph aloud.

Name ______________________________ Date ______________

The Reel World

The word wheels below contain ten movie terms. Separate the letters into ten words. Then write each of the ten words on the line next to its correct definition.

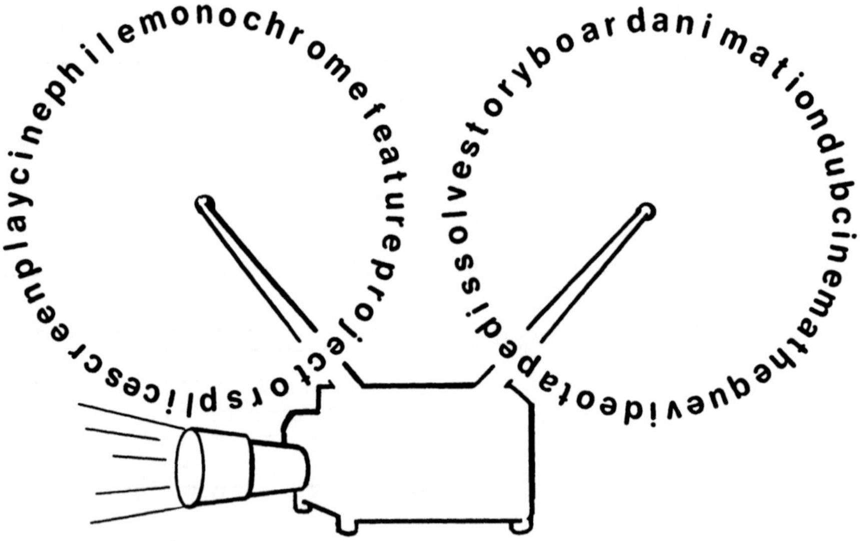

screenplaycinephilemonochromefeatureprojectorsplices

dissolvestoryboardanimationdubcinemathequevideotape

______________ 1. a small movie house specializing in avant-garde films

______________ 2. characterized by the reproduction of visual images in tones of gray

______________ 3. the script (and possibly shooting directions) of a story prepared for motion-picture production

______________ 4. a gradual superimposing of one picture upon another on a screen

______________ 5. a machine that causes film images to appear on a screen

______________ 6. a recording of a movie (or television production) on magnetic tape

______________ 7. the act of photographing successive positions of drawings or other inanimate subjects so as to give them movement

______________ 8. the principal motion picture shown on a program with other subjects

______________ 9. a series of panels of small rough drawings showing changes of scene and action in a planned film

______________ 10. a devotee of motion pictures

______________ 11. to unite two pieces of film by lapping two ends together

______________ 12. to add sound effects or new dialogue to a film

Movie Analysis On a separate sheet of paper, write a two-page report on a recent movie you have seen. Analyze the movie, including a discussion of the character, plot, motivation, conflict, and theme.

Name ______________________________ Date ______________

Word Fun

First, define each term below. (You may use a dictionary.) Then, write the letter of the word next to the word or phrase below that is an example of it.

a. **pun** ______________________________

____

b. **palindrome** ______________________________

____

c. **oxymoron** ______________________________

____

d. **anagram** ______________________________

____

e. **neologism** ______________________________

____

f. **nonce word** ______________________________

____

g. **malapropism** ______________________________

____

h. **spoonerism** ______________________________

____

i. **litotes** ______________________________

____

j. **hyperbole** ______________________________

_______ 1. wise fool; jumbo shrimp

_______ 2. Ramona Clay secretly wrote romance novels under the pseudonym Clara Monay.

_______ 3. brillig; Jabberwock

_______ 4. "Madam, I'm Adam."

_______ 5. biofeedback; picosecond

_______ 6. The sports announcer meant to speak of a crushing blow, but instead he shouted, "It was a blushing crow if I ever saw one!"

_______ 7. "They went and told the sexton and the sexton tolled the bell."

_______ 8. Did she fully reprehend the meaning of the word?

_______ 9. The chef's biscuits were harder than the Rock of Gibraltar.

_______ 10. Not a bad general, George Washington led the Colonials to victory.

Etymology Etymology is the study of words. How many words can you make out of the letters in ***etymology***? On a separate sheet of paper, try to list at least twenty-five such words.

Name ______________________________ Date ______________

Family Words

Adopt, ancestors, brother, child, clan, cousin, daughter, divorce, father, genealogy, generation, grandparents, kinship, marriage, matrilinear, monogamous, mother, patrilinear, polyandry, polygamy, relative, sibling, sister, son, spouse – these twenty-five words are hidden below. They run from left to right or from top to bottom. Circle each of the hidden words. Then list the four words that apply to males only and the five words that apply to females only in the space provided below. You may use a dictionary.

```
A B C D M H G F E J A D O P T I K L P N
M P O U O Q R S E T V W A X Y Z W G V T
S A R Q N U M O P O L Y G A M Y N R P I
J T K L O H G F E A B C D E F G H A J K
C R L I G D A U G H T E R J K K O N M N
H I P U A Q N R S C L A N E I T M D V W
I L A X M Y C Z W S P L S O N H A P D R
L I A E O I E O U E A X T Q S M R A J E
D N F B U C S G K N R V Y Z H Y R R X L
A E E T S V T W F A T H E R I U I E Q A
R A S O M N O P I J K L E F P G A N H T
A R B C D H R C O U S I N G F E G T I I
O M N P L K S J I E F G H D C B E S G V
A E F G H M A T R I L I N E A R I J E E
K L S P O U S E P N M O U Q R S P N N M
M O T H E R O I J K L P N M O S R Q E U
E T U W Z Y X A E U D I V O R C E Q R R
S W V T E A X Y Z W S P L H D A E F A M
H L G E N E A L O G Y K S I S T E R T N
B R O T H E R R V W X T Q M J F B A I E
I J M Q R X V P O L Y A N D R Y R N O K
G C S I B L I N G A D H L P S U W R N N
```

Words that apply to males only:

____

____

____

____

Words that apply to females only:

____

____

____

____

____

Family Tree Make a family tree of your family. Include at least three generations.

Name ______________________________ Date ______________

The Self

Read each sentence below and think about the definition of the boldfaced word. Circle **T** if a statement is true. Circle **F** if it is false. If the sentence is false, write a correct definition of the boldfaced word on the back of this sheet of paper. You may use a dictionary.

T F 1. **Behavior** is the complex of characteristics that distinguishes an individual.

T F 2. A **demure** person is modest and reserved.

T F 3. A person who accomplishes too much is an **overachiever**.

T F 4. **Delusion** is the perception of objects that have no reality, usually arising from a disorder of the nervous system or in response to drugs.

T F 5. Excitement, mental and physical hyperactivity, disorganization of behavior, and elevation of mood is **mania**.

T F 6. **Personality** is the manner of conducting oneself, the response of an individual to her or his environment.

T F 7. To be **flippant** is to be superficial, talkative, and lacking proper respect or seriousness.

T F 8. A persistent false belief regarding the self or objects outside the self is a **hallucination**.

T F 9. To **self-actualize** is to realize fully one's potential.

T F 10. **Psychosis** is the ability to foresee the future.

T F 11. The diverting of an instinct or impulse from its more primitive form to a more socially acceptable form is called **sublimation**.

T F 12. An **inhibition** is a court order prohibiting the sale or use of alcoholic beverages.

Psychiatric Words Across the top of a sheet of paper, print the word ***psychiatric***. Number the sheet of paper from 1–25. Make at least twenty-five other words from the letters in the word ***psychiatric***. (How far beyond twenty-five can you go?)

Name ______________________________ Date ______________

Legal Terms

v e r d i c t j u s t i c e d e p o s i t i o n s e n t e n c e j u r y

Separate the letters at the top and bottom of this page into ten words. Then write the correct word on each line below. You may use a dictionary.

1. To free or clear from a charge or an accusation is to ________________ .
2. A(n) ________________ is the decision reached by a jury at the end of a trial.
3. A(n) ________________ is a written statement (testimony under oath) by a witness for use in court.
4. A law enacted by a legislature is a(n) ________________ .
5. ________________ is the deliberate giving of false or misleading testimony under oath.
6. A written declaration made under oath before a notary public or other authorized official is a(n) ________________ .
7. A court judgment, a(n) ________________ is the decision of what punishment is due a convicted person.
8. A(n) ________________ is a court order prohibiting a party from a specific course of action.
9. To call somebody before a court to answer an accusation is to ________________ .
10. Fair, impartial, and morally right treatment is ________________

a r r a i g n s t a t u t e a c q u i t i n j u n c t i o n a f f i d a v i t

Legal News From a newspaper, clip several articles about legal matters. Circle all the legal terms. Define at least three such terms that do not appear in the words above.

Name ______________________________ Date ______________

Work Compounds

Each work word on this page is a compound word—one word made out of two separate words (such as *gold* + *fish* = *goldfish*). Make the words for twelve work terms by combining one word from the left-hand box with one word from the right-hand box.

down	**work**	**burn**
in-	**low**	**labor-**
flex	**jury-**	**blue-**
hard	**head**	**green-**

hat	**time**	**intensive**
rig	**load**	**carder**
out	**time**	**hunter**
ball	**house**	**collar**

__________ 1. exhaustion of physical or emotional strength

__________ 2. a construction worker

__________ 3. describes work or projects carried on within an organization

__________ 4. to give a customer a deceptively low price or cost estimate

__________ 5. refers to industrial workers, especially semiskilled and unskilled labor

__________ 6. period during which a machine or factory is shut down

__________ 7. to put something together for temporary use

__________ 8. the amount of work assigned for completion in a given time

__________ 9. system in which employees can choose their working hours

__________ 10. an alien granted permission to reside and work in the United States

__________ 11. requiring a large labor force and small investment in capital goods

__________ 12. agent specializing in recruitment of highly skilled workers or managers

New Compounds On a separate sheet of paper, use the word parts above to invent six new compound words (for example, *in-hat*) about work. Define each of your new words and use each one in a sentence.

Name ______________________ Date ______________

Style and Slang

Below are ten scrambled words referring to style. Read each brief definition. Then unscramble the word and write it on the line. You may use a dictionary.

1. sunglasses	**asdehs**	_ _ _ _ _ _
2. pants, usually jeans, made into shorts by cutting off the legs	**ftocsuf**	_ _ _ _ _ _ _
3. to extract useful materials from waste	**cyrcele**	_ _ _ _ _ _ _
4. exaggerated, inflated claims, especially in advertising	**peyh**	_ _ _ _
5. to braid hair close to the scalp in rows	**onrworc**	_ _ _ _ _ _ _
6. a distinctive aura, feeling, or atmosphere	**amark**	_ _ _ _ _
7. designed to be discarded after use	**arawhotyw**	_ _ _ _ _ _ _ _ _
8. attracting attention in a showy, gaudy, or pretentious way	**tilzyg**	_ _ _ _ _ _
9. unimportant things	**avirit**	_ _ _ _ _ _
10. long thin braids of hair worn by Rastafarians or reggae musicians	**dodcrealsk**	_ _ _ _ _ _ _ _ _ _

Slang List Slang words are often only temporary additions to our language; many of them come and go in a few years, to be replaced by new slang terms. On the back of this sheet of paper, make a list of ten current slang terms. Define each.

Name ______________________ Date ____________

Educational Words

Write an answer to each question below. You may use the dictionary.

1. What is the difference between a **college** and a **university**? ____________

2. What is the difference between **dyslexia** and **dysgraphia**? ____________

3. Write two definitions of the word **preppie**.

   (a) ____________

   (b) ____________

4. What is the difference between a **teacher** and a **tutor**? ____________

5. What does **dogmatic** mean? ____________

6. What is a **pedant**? ____________

7. Define:

   (a) **alumna** ____________

   (b) **alumnae** ____________

   (c) **alumnus** ____________

   (d) **alumni** ____________

Humanities Currently there is much discussion in education over a return to the humanities, which have been overshadowed by science and business courses. On a separate sheet of paper, define the term ***humanities***. Then write a paragraph arguing for or against the teaching of humanities.

Name ______________________________ Date ______________

Political Words

Fill in the blanks below by writing the correct word on each line. You may use a dictionary.

schism	**suffrage**	**imperialism**	**coup d'état**
reprisal	**deregulate**	**demagogue**	**incrementalism**
treason	**ombudsman**	**gerrymander**	**decriminalize**

1. ________________ is the offense of attempting to overthrow the government of the state of which one is a citizen.
2. To remove previous government restrictions is to ________________ .
3. A leader who makes use of popular prejudices, a(n) ________________ makes promises in order to gain power.
4. A(n) ________________ is a division or separation.
5. A policy of advocating political or social change by degrees is ________________ .
6. To ________________ is to remove or reduce the classification of an act as an illegal offense.
7. The governmental act of resorting to force short of war in retaliation for damages or loss suffered is ________________ .
8. The violent overthrow of an existing government by a small group is a(an) ________________ .
9. ________________ is the policy of extending the power of a nation by acquiring territories or by gaining indirect control over the political or economic life of other areas.
10. A(n) ________________ is an appointed official who investigates reported complaints from the public and who helps achieve settlement.
11. To ________________ is to divide an area into electoral districts so as to give one political party an electoral advantage.
12. The right of voting is called ________________ .

More Political Terms On the back of this sheet of paper, define the following terms: **dark horse, featherbedding, lame duck, muckraker, mudslinger, pork barrel.**

Name ______________________ Date ______________

Myth Words

Twelve words are hidden below, one in each line. Read each clue; then circle the one word in each row that goes with the clue. You may use a dictionary.

Clue	Letters
1. from Egyptian myth, a bird that lived 500 years, then consumed itself in fire, rising again from its own ashes	A K A P H O E N I X B O F M D
2. in Greek legend, monster with body of man and head of bull	B M I N O T A U R U S X O R J
3. mythical animal with body and hind legs of lion and head and wings of eagle	H I N J P O R V G R I F F I N
4. in Norse myth, great hall where souls of heroes feast	T U V A L H A L L A W Y X E N
5. in Arthurian legend, King Arthur's sword	G E F E X C A L I B U R M I D
6. in Hindu legend, incarnation of god Vishnu; now means any terrible, irresistible force	G I N J U G G E R N A U T U S
7. in Greek legend, fire-breathing monster with lion's head, goat's body, and serpent's tail	C H I M E R A Q U X V O R T U
8. in Greek myth, a race of female warriors	D F A M A M A Z O N S J O W Y
9. from Greek myth, a nine-headed serpent	C L G E F M I N H I H Y D R A
10. in Greek legend, a Titan who supported the heavens on his shoulders	M I A T L A S S V O R Y T U W
11. in Old English legend, a warrior who slew a monster and reigned as king	G C L B E F B E O W U L F I N
12. the monster slain by the above hero	P E G E N F I G R E N D E L M

Monster Headlines On a separate sheet of paper, write twelve headlines. Each headline should use one of the monster words from above. Try to write headlines about current events and/or sports.

Name ______________________________ Date ______________

Economic Rhyme

Read each definition below. Write the answer on the line. The answer rhymes with the boldfaced word. (Remember that words which rhyme are not always spelled similarly.) You may use the dictionary.

1. A compulsory payment the government levies on income, property, sales price, and such to support itself.
   Rhymes with **jacks**. _ _ _

2. A medium of exchange stamped by government authority.
   Rhymes with **funny**. _ _ _ _ _

3. Taxes placed by a government on imported items.
   Rhymes with **sheriff**. _ _ _ _ _ _

4. A temporary falling off of business activity.
   Rhymes with **impression**. _ _ _ _ _ _ _ _ _

5. An increase in the amount of money in circulation, resulting in a sudden fall in value and a rise in prices.
   Rhymes with **location**. _ _ _ _ _ _ _ _ _

6. The amount of money asked or paid for something.
   Rhymes with **vise**. _ _ _ _ _

7. A person who buys goods or services for his own needs.
   Rhymes with **perfumer**. _ _ _ _ _ _ _ _

8. The buying and selling of commodities.
   Rhymes with **paid**. _ _ _ _ _

9. The barest means of making a living in terms of food, clothing, and shelter needed to sustain life.
   Rhymes with **insistence**. _ _ _ _ _ _ _ _ _ _ _

10. A period of slackening business, widespread unemployment, falling prices, and falling wages.
    Rhymes with **impression**. _ _ _ _ _ _ _ _ _ _

Economic Terms On a separate sheet of paper, define the following terms: **cost-effective, double-dipper, megabucks, petrodollars, poor-mouth, red-line.**

Name ______________________________ Date ______________

More Legal Terms

Read each brief definition or description. Circle the one word from the three boldfaced words that best matches the definition. You may use a dictionary.

1. having made no legal will	**intestate**	**bequest**	**draconian**
2. to deprive somebody of a right of citizenship	**codicil**	**appellate**	**disenfranchise**
3. goods that it is against the law to import or export	**larceny**	**collusion**	**contraband**
4. the unlawful beating of another person	**assault**	**battery**	**larceny**
5. to take money for one's own use in violation of a trust	**abscond**	**embezzle**	**abnegate**
6. the legal surrender of an alleged criminal to the jurisdiction of another body	**equity**	**acquittal**	**extradition**
7. the taking and removing of another person's personal property unlawfully	**abscond**	**larceny**	**tort**
8. the unlawful killing of a human being without intent to do injury	**corpus**	**murder**	**manslaughter**
9. a supplement or appendix to a will	**codicil**	**tort**	**extradition**
10. the right and power to interpret and apply the law	**habeas**	**litigation**	**jurisdiction**
11. a court of justice	**tribunal**	**tort**	**jurisprudence**
12. a secret agreement between two or more persons for a deceitful or fraudulent purpose	**collusion**	**draconian**	**abnegation**

Undefined Terms From the list above, choose five undefined terms. Then, on the back of this sheet of paper, define each of the five.

Name ______________________________ Date ______________

Willing to Work

Read the ad below. Then, in the space provided, write each of the boldfaced words. Next to each word, write its definition. You may use a dictionary.

WANTED!
Young Men and Women,
Energetic and Eager to Work!

We offer every job imaginable:
Internist
Lapidary
Dermatologist!
We mix the common with the uncommon,
the highly skilled with the semiskilled.
Entomologist
Farrier
Roustabout!
We offer the calm and the cool and the collected.
We offer the wild, the exciting, the adventuous.
Ornithologist
Stenographer
Cooper!
Don't despair. There's a job waiting just for you!
Hod Carrier
Pedicurist
Etymologist!

1. ______________________________
2. ______________________________
3. ______________________________
4. ______________________________
5. ______________________________
6. ______________________________
7. ______________________________
8. ______________________________
9. ______________________________
10. ______________________________
11. ______________________________
12. ______________________________

Jobs A–Z Number a separate sheet of paper from 1 through 26. Label each line with a letter of the alphabet, A–Z. Try to list one job for each of the letters of the alphabet. (Do not use any of the twelve job names above.)

Name ______________________ Date ______________

Social Issues

The word wheel below contains ten words dealing with social issues. Separate the letters into ten words. Then write each of the ten words on the line next to its correct definition.

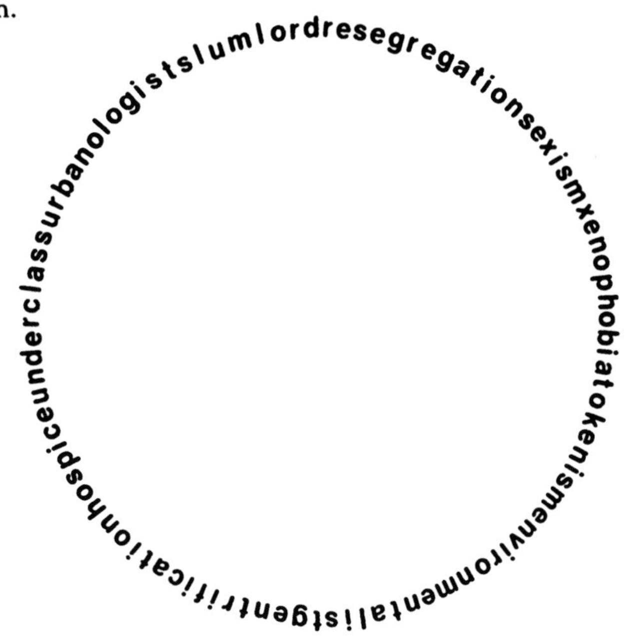

slumlordresegregationsexismxenophobiatokenismenvironmentalistgentrificationhospiceunderclassurbanologists

________ 1. a fear of or contempt of strangers or foreigners

________ 2. a program or place that provides for the needs of terminally ill patients

________ 3. a person who specializes in city problems

________ 4. a renewal of the policy of separation of one group from another after a period of integration

________ 5. discrimination based on sex

________ 6. a person who seeks to protect our natural surroundings.

________ 7. the lowest social and economic strata in society

________ 8. the restoration of deteriorated urban property by the middle and upper classes

________ 9. the policy of making only a symbolic gesture toward the accomplishment of a goal

________ 10. a landlord of slum property

Social Issues On a separate sheet of paper, write a three-paragraph essay on the three most important social issues you as an individual will face in your lifetime. What are they, how will they affect you, what is your attitude toward them, and what do you think should be done about them? (Possible social issues include: employment/unemployment; job quality; social diseases; war; poverty; discrimination; parenting; education, etc.)

Name ______________________________ Date ______________

More Myth Words

Each sentence below is missing three parts: (a) a history, (b) a derivative word, (c) a definition. Fill in the missing parts of each sentence by choosing an answer from each of the three columns and writing the answers on the line. You may use a dictionary.

1. Odysseus was ______ , from whose name we get the word ______________ which means ______ .
2. Styx was ______ , from whose name we get the word ______________ which means ______ .
3. Phobos was ______ , from whose name we get the word ______________ which means ______ .
4. Ceres was ______ , from whose name we get the word ______________ which means ______ .
5. A Myrmidon was ______ , from whose name we get the word ______________ which means ______ .
6. Proteus was ______ , from whose name we get the word ______________ which means ______ .
7. Mars was ______ , from whose name we get the word ______________ which means ______ .
8. Procrustes was ______ , from whose name we get the word ______________ which means ______ .

a. the river over which the souls of the dead were ferried

b. any of a tribe of warriors who fought with Achilles at Troy

c. the Roman god of war

d. king of Ithaca; a leader of the Trojan War

e. a sea god who could change his shape or appearance

f. a giant who seized travelers, tied them to a bed frame, then stretched them or cut off their limbs so that they would fit

g. an attendant of the Greek god Ares

h. the Roman goddess of agriculture

cereal

myrmidon

stygian

procrustean

phobia

odyssey

martial

protean

s. an irrational, persistent fear of some particular thing

t. an extended wandering or journey

u. pertaining to war; warlike

v. any grain used for food

w. very changeable

x. dark or gloomy; infernal

y. designed to or acting to achieve conformity at any cost; drastic

z. an unquestioning follower or subordinate

Stop Hectoring Me At the library, use a book on mythology or a special dictionary to look up these words: **hector, gorgon, thespian, plutonian, tantalize, narcissism, furies, muses.** On a separate sheet of paper, write the words. After each word, write a paragraph explaining the origins of the word and its meaning.